# The Politics an
# Kathl

MARIE MULHOLLAND

Plate 1: Signed plate of Kathleen Lynn given by her as a memento in 1936 to her friend and comrade, Brigid Davis. *Courtesy of Kilmainham Gaol and Museum*.

ACTIVIST TO ACTIVIST

*Editor* Ruth Taillon

# THE POLITICS AND RELATIONSHIPS *of* KATHLEEN LYNN

MARIE MULHOLLAND

The Woodfield Press

This book was typeset by
Red Barn Publishing, Skeagh, Co. Cork for
THE WOODFIELD PRESS
17 Jamestown Square, Dublin 8
www.woodfield-press.com
e-mail: terri.mcdonnell@ireland.com

Publishing Editor
Helen Harnett

House Editor
Florence Esson



A catalogue record for this title
is available from the British Library.

ISBN 0-9534293-2-6



Printed in Ireland
by ColourBooks, Dublin

# CONTENTS

ACKNOWLEDGMENTS

Like any ambition achieved, this book was the product of enormous faith and wonderful generosity. In my particular circumstances, those essential contributions were provided by a number of women, any one of whom it would be a privilege to know; but to have them all pulling together for me, well it just doesn't get any better than this.

My publisher's faith in me was so unwavering it was scarey, and consequently Terri McDonnell never had to nag or cajole — my fear of letting her down was motivation enough. Helen Harnett's confidence in Kathleen's story and my ability to tell it was contagious and without it I would never have gotten this far. Ruth Taillon was my choice of editor and I never had reason to regret that decision. Katherine O'Donnell was the source of light that allowed me to look beyond the shadows at both Kathleen and myself. Jane Pillinger did what she has always done, loved me and affirmed me throughout all my endeavours; perhaps only Kathleen herself could appreciate the full worth of such support.

# Foreword

This is the first volume in the *Activist to Activist* series. The series will comprise of a collection of biographical studies focusing on the involvement of women in Irish public life or public life abroad. While we are sure that the series will be of interest to a wide general readership, these books are intended to do more than encourage intellectual curiosity about Irish women's history. We hope that in publishing these short studies on Irish women's lives, we can ensure their legacy is a continuing influence on the thinking and work of today's female activists — and, through them, on social, political and economic developments in Ireland today. Our authors are themselves women involved in Irish public life or Irish women activists working in other countries. They may be involved in community or electoral politics, the trade union movement, or the women's movement. Perhaps they are or have been active in campaigning for social reforms, civil liberties or human rights or on environmental issues. Through this book, and the volumes to follow, they will reflect on their own experiences to bring new perspectives to the lives of their subjects.

It is appropriate that the first subject in the series is Dr Kathleen Lynn. Dr Lynn is today remembered primarily for her outstanding contributions in the field of children's medicine and for her involvement in the Easter Rising of 1916. Although her name is frequently mentioned, detail of her work has been sparse.

We have known even less about the private side of Kathleen's life and Marie Mulholland has broken important new ground with the work presented here.

Kathleen Lynn was one of many young educated Irish Protestant women who, in the early years of the twentieth century, found themselves identifying with the progressive cultural, social and political movements of the day. They were women who, by virtue of their class position, had the economic independence that enabled them to involve themselves in political and social activism. Their educational advantage also gave them the intellectual and social skills that sometimes allowed them to move into positions of leadership. We remember them today, partly because their qualities of leadership and contribution to movements for social change were recognised and noted by their contemporaries. We are also able to reconstruct —however imperfectly — the lives of women like Kathleen because they also left behind a documented record of their own lives. While celebrating the legacy of women like Kathleen, it is important to remember that the contributions and achievements of many of her sister comrades have been lost to us simply because their social standing precluded the documentation of their lives.

Kathleen, like many of her contemporaries, came first to an awareness of the need to challenge the mores of a patriarchal society that refused her equality with men. Her intellectual rigour and her sensitivity to the suffering and struggles of others led her to generalise this understanding to a holistic socialist-feminist analysis. Her strength of character required her to act on the basis of her analysis and to involve herself in a wide range of political organisations and work for social reform. Like her friend and comrade Constance Markievicz, Kathleen sacrificed many of the privileges enjoyed by other women of similar social background when she aligned herself with the disadvantaged and oppressed. A much greater sacrifice than the loss of economic security and physical comforts, however, was the estrangement from family and other close personal relationships.

Marie Mulholland's exploration of Kathleen's personal and political relationships has been so successful because she brings to it the insight of her own life as both an activist and a lesbian feminist. She is able to read between the lines and fill in the gaps of Kathleen's life by interpreting it through the prism of her own experience. Just as importantly, her telling of the story of Kathleen Lynn draws out the lessons and historical parallels for those of us who are activists today.

My path first crossed that of Marie Mulholland in 1978 at a women's liberation conference in England. I was a young feminist who had recently arrived in Britain from Canada. Marie was an even younger feminist who had recently arrived from Ireland. Marie came to my notice when she took the floor in anger to demand of English feminists that they oppose the British government's war in Ireland. Over the years our paths would continue to cross many times, particularly after we both came to settle permanently in Ireland. Marie's involvement in a wide array of causes and campaigns — as a trade unionist, a feminist, a lesbian, a socialist, and a Republican — has been tireless. To this she has now added the label of a historian. While her analytical skills have been honed, her passion remains undiminished. Like Kathleen Lynn before her, perhaps she too will encourage by her example a new generation of women activists.

*To*

Kerry Flynn and Orlaith Mulholland in the hope that they will never have to search for their own history as Irishwomen.

**Also published by The Woodfield Press**

*The Wicklow World of Elizabeth Smith (1840–1850)*
DERMOT JAMES and SÉAMAS Ó MAITIÚ, Editors

*The Sligo-Leitrim World of Kate Cullen (1832–1913)*
revealed by HILARY PYLE

*Ballyknockan: A Wicklow Stonecutters' Village*
SÉAMAS Ó MAITIÚ and BARRY O'REILLY

*The Tellicherry Five: The Transportation of Michael Dwyer and the Wicklow Rebels*
KIERAN SHEEDY

*John Hamilton of Donegal 1800–1884: This Recklessly Generous Landlord*
DERMOT JAMES

*Red-Headed Rebel: A Biography of Susan Mitchell*
HILARY PYLE

*Charles Dickens' Ireland: An Anthology*
JIM COOKE

*Faith or Fatherhood? Bishop Dunboyne's Dilemma –*
*The Story of John Butler, Catholic Bishop of Cork 1763–1787*
CON COSTELLO

W & R Jacob: Celebrating 150 Years of Irish Biscuit Making
SÉAMAS Ó MAITIÚ

*Female Activists: Irish Women and Change (1900–1960)*
MARY CULLEN and MARIA LUDDY, Editors

# Introduction

# Re-Discovering Kathleen Lynn

In 1987, I was presented with the Constance Markievicz award[1] by the Irish-American Labour Coalition of the AFL-CIO, Boston, for services to the community as a trade unionist. In an effort to fully appreciate the award given to me in the name of the Countess, I immersed myself in material that would develop my knowledge of her beyond the stuff of popular legend. My enjoyment of Constance remains undiminished, but the name of Kathleen Lynn kept 'bobbing up', particularly in Diana Norman's biography of Markievicz, which was published that same year.[2] Kathleen appeared to be present at all the most significant moments in the history of early twentieth-century Irish nationalism; but, frustratingly, her name would appear and just as quickly disappear without explanation. Over the years since then, I have gone from wondering, 'Who is this woman?' to 'Why have historians given her life and work so little attention?'.

The answer to this is perhaps that Kathleen, like her friend Constance, does not sit easily within the accepted male versions of Irish history, being neither an appendage to a man nor a victim. Neither does she fit into certain feminist readings of history, because her involvement with the nationalist movement has been perceived to undermine her feminist credentials. Nevertheless, I offer this necessarily restricted exploration of Kathleen's politics and relationships as the history of an Irish republican feminist, because without the historical contribution

1 I was the first recipient of the Constance Markievicz Award for services to my community as a trade unionist, presented by the Irish American Labour Coalition of the AFL-CIO, Boston, USA on 4 June 1987.

2 Diana Norman, *Terrible Beauty, A Life of Constance Markievicz*, 1987.

of women like Kathleen, my own identity as an Irish Republican feminist would have no precedent.

## Feminism and Republicanism

For feminists, Irish republicanism has always been akin to having a relationship with an unfaithful partner. We are attracted to republicanism because of its compatibility with our need for equality within the creation of a state promising equality for all. So we pursue those ambitions – balancing our needs as women with the need to pull together to end British domination and partition – attempting to forge an equal partnership between republicanism and feminism. The problems arise because republicans see their relationship with feminism as just one more string to their bow. It is another obligation they intend to honour, but one that is not considered to necessitate any political recalibration in pursuit of the primary objective, the overthrow of British imperialism in Ireland.

From Cumann na dTeachtaire[3] to Clár na mBan, feminist republicans have had to assert their right to be recognised as equals at the negotiating table and in the decision-making processes of republicanism. Kathleen fought in Cumann na dTeachtaire (the League of Women Delegates) for women's representation on the Sinn Féin executive in 1918. In 1995, Republican feminists including myself felt driven to establish Clár na mBan (the Women's Agenda) to press for women's inclusion in the Peace Process. Clár na mBan argued for women's representation in the Sinn Féin negotiating team and raised the concerns that women wanted addressed within a negotiated settlement.

It has been my experience that in order to prevent women's rights slipping off the Republican agenda, women need to apply pressure both within and outside the movement. Too

3 Cumann na dTeachtaire, also known as the League of Women Delegates, was a caucus of Republican feminists intent on recognition of women's equal status within Sinn Féin. Details of its origins and actions are contained in Chapter 4.

often, both in past and contemporary times, women's energies within republicanism have been conscripted into the priority of the moment: armed resistance, prison struggles, elections and hunger strikes. That these were crucial campaigns in the political strategies of republicans and, more importantly, for the simple survival of the whole nationalist community is not in question here. The dedication and diligence with which women took part in, promoted and delivered those campaigns has not, however, been proportionately reciprocated by the Republican movement's endorsement of women's rights. This reality does not motivate me to abandon support for republicanism, only to recognise the shortcomings of many of its proponents. Indeed the history of republicanism's fair-weather attitude to women's equality only confirms the necessity for feminism to retain its autonomy to act on its own behalf, whilst also acting in concert and solidarity with other movements when expedient to do so.

## Writing women's history

The necessity of writing women's history has been cogently argued by feminist historians.[4] The movement to reclaim women and their agency in history is a developing one, and there are still significant gaps in our knowledge about many individual women, their organisations, activities and contributions to society. Kathleen Lynn is one woman who has, until recently, fallen through the cracks. Fortunately, two women historians, Medb Ruane and Dr Margaret O'hÓgartaigh, are currently rescuing her from the undergrowth of historical footnotes. The latter is preparing a full biography focusing on Kathleen's medical career soon to be published by Cork University Press. With the publication of these two books, Kathleen Lynn will hopefully gain the historical prominence she richly deserves.

4 Mary Cullen, 'History Women and History Men' in *History Ireland* (Summer, 1994) pp. 31–36; Gerda Lerner, 'Placing Women in History: A 1975 Perspective' in Berenice A. Carroll (ed.), *Liberating Women's History* (Illinois, 1976). These are a sample and not a definitive list.

In writing of the need to give historical attention to nationalist and feminist women, Margaret Ward points out that with:

> . . . nationalist women the task is easier because the landmarks [of the nationalist cause] have been defined and so the task becomes one of finding the evidence to describe the important role we all suspected, but could not document, that women had played during the various stages of the struggle against British rule in Ireland.[5]

The 'task of finding evidence' in relation to Kathleen was alleviated to some extent by the availability of her personal diaries, which span almost 40 years.[6] The period under examination here does, however, also cover a time that precedes the scope of the diaries. It is concentrated on the most politically active period of Kathleen's life: from her membership of the Irish Women's Suffrage and Local Government Association in 1903 to the formation of Fianna Fáil in 1926. This period represents only a fraction of the contribution that she made to Irish society over her lifetime and, in particular, refers only in passing to the enormous strides she took in the field of Irish medicine and paediatrics. The focus of my research has been to examine the private/public dichotomy in Kathleen's life. Her diary entries have been utilised to enlighten my understanding of her personal involvements; but they are frustratingly brief, often cryptic and, unless otherwise identified, normally free of any political analysis or personal reflection. Kathleen left clues, but never direct explanations.

Participation in public life did not cease for Kathleen in 1926, but that year heralded her full-time commitment to the development of St Ultan's Hospital and the re-moulding of her destiny at a stage in her life when she chose to direct her auton-

5 Margaret Ward, 'The Missing Sex: Putting Women into History' in *A Dozen Lips* (Dublin, 1991) p. 219.

6 Kathleen Lynn's transcribed diaries from 1916 to the year of her death in 1955 are held in the Royal College of Physicians, Dublin. I am indebted to the College's librarian, Robert Mills, for always providing me with generous access to them during my research.

omy towards a goal of self-fulfilment. It seems fitting then to end my exploration at a place in Kathleen's life where I am just arriving.

## Republican feminism in today's Ireland

The present political state of affairs in Ireland is still too unpredictable and raw to allow the kind of reflections required for me to make sense of the last 30 years and my role within it for over 20 of those. The struggle for justice and equality on this island has taken so many new forms, and opposition to that struggle has found more subtle and pernicious weapons than bullets and bombs.

At the time of writing, little girls in Ardoyne (to one of whom this book is dedicated) face a harrowing journey to school confronted daily by a hatred that was allowed to flourish in a state founded on exclusion and sectarianism. With that state endangered by the advent of democracy, small children have become the prime enemy because they symbolise the confidence of a future Ireland without partition.

In the cities and towns of Ireland, the people who fled here for refuge and for a future, or those simply needing a halting site, are spat at, assaulted and rejected by the insularity and selfishness of de Valera's successors. The mythical purity of Ireland is threatened by the determination of new Irish generations to take root and thrive.

I think Kathleen would have welcomed the possibilities converging in Ireland, represented by the children of Ardoyne and the new peoples within its shores. I feel that her Republican feminism would have propelled her into action to ensure safe passage for the schoolgirls of North Belfast, and the humanitarian internationalist would have defied her own government to assert the rights of minorities. Kathleen's life and priorities provide a reality check that sustains my own endeavours, and provides necessary encouragement to increase them when faced with the hypocrisy and political self-interest that haunts the struggle for equality in Ireland today. In that sense Kathleen Lynn is my touchstone, an historical legacy left to me that clarifies my present; yet the decision on how best to proceed into the future is my own.

The roles and positions of women in Ireland may have diversified with the securing of many rights denied to Kathleen and her contemporaries, but still today our presence is contained and our power conditional. If a reminder of women's continued existence on the margins of real power is required, then we need look no further than the drama unfolding on the world stage at the end of 2001. As the curtain lifts on a new and more frightening display of supremacy, the cast still reads like a testament to testosterone: Bush, Blair, Bin Laden, Powell, the Taliban, Sharon, Berlusconi *et al.*

The decisions on how to contribute to the future of this island and how to maintain an alternative response to global abuse of power are ones I make within the context of possible alliances, shared politics, common principles and recognisable affinities. In much the same way that Kathleen chose her allegiances and comrades, I continue to choose mine and do not always expect to finish the journey with all of the same company.

Kathleen's life and my own life have taught me to appreciate that the consistency of political fellow travellers is both possible and precious. Perhaps this is my ultimate attraction to Kathleen: she was a sister traveller and – despite our differing class backgrounds and educational beginnings – I find her footsteps have so often preceded my own. Republican feminism is not yet so well-trodden a path that I can ignore the signposts left by those responsible for its first navigation.

## Relationships between women

In placing a spotlight on Kathleen's relationships with women, I reflect my own preoccupations, in the same way that my examination of her republicanism and feminism coincide with my political priorities. Strangely but unsurprisingly, when I first became interested in Kathleen I had little knowledge of her relationship with Madeleine ffrench-Mullen. I thought only that Madeleine, like several other contemporaries, was Kathleen's comrade and feminist sister. I say unsurprisingly, because in contemporary times I rarely encounter other Republican feminists who also claim and act upon attractions for women. Thus, I never dreamed of finding my reflection in an earlier, even more sexually divided Ireland than the one I came out to in 1980.

In exploring Kathleen's relationship with Madeleine, I threw myself into an academic wrestling match; that is, the debate on whether women from a past century whose domestic and intimate lives revolved around other women could be described as lesbian, and whether those intimacies took sexual expression. Were eroticised affections merely the romantic outlet permitted to women without men and hence insignificant? Were intense lifelong commitments between emancipated women the only relationships available to them that could support their feminist aspirations and political involvements? Was an enduring affection between two spinsters a positive alternative to the confinement of traditional nineteenth and early twentieth-century marriage? On and on it went, and deeper and deeper I fell into the quagmire of categories, contradictions, conditions and contexts that were posited as the relevant criteria to establish if Kathleen and Madeleine were lovers.

As one friend and enormous source of encouragement remarked, 'what do they want, the bedroom film?' She was right. I was falling into the trap of believing that I must provide incontrovertible evidence of Kathleen and Madeleine's physical relationship, while for heterosexual biographers and their heterosexual subjects the assumption of heterosexuality appears to suffice. So, without lurid descriptions of sexual activities or photographs of the subjects in compromising positions, where is the evidence of the true nature of Kathleen's relationship with Madeleine?

The evidence is found throughout the emotional, professional, public and private dimensions of Kathleen's life and is rarely hidden. Madeleine and Kathleen were regarded as a team by friends, comrades and colleagues. The scale of their political and professional achievements, and the lifetime consistency of their efforts together and separately, would daunt even the modern-day activist, despite the modern benefits of computers, email, mobile phones and faster transport. To maintain such range and depth of commitment requires an unlimited source of sustenance and support, such as emanates only from the most intimate, shared knowledge and mutual empathy.

Kathleen's diaries contain frank and loving references to Madeleine that are at odds with her often dispassionate accounts of revolutionary and otherwise extraordinary events and undertakings. For instance, in the days following Easter Sunday 1916, Kathleen declared her preference for an overcrowded, unsanitary prison cell shared with Madeleine to the relative comfort of the Mountjoy cell to which she was later transferred. Evidence of the loving domestic environment that Kathleen and Madeleine created is found in Kathleen's diary. There are many touching references to shared breakfasts. Extracts about anticipated homecomings, after extended periods apart due to family visits, hospital stays or enforced separations because of political or military activities, are charged with barely suppressed excitement.

The medical and social constructs placed on women's relationships would have seriously impeded any explicit acknowledgment of sexual intimacy. Combined with their own discretion and desire for privacy, women like Kathleen would have been extremely circumspect in the conduct of their personal and intimate relationships with female partners. As Donoghue asserts, these influences, 'as well as the censoring actions of families and scholars, would have ensured that most passions between women were presented in letters and memoirs as harmless and innocent'.[7]

Ruane believes that Kathleen's unwavering Christianity and adherence to the Church of Ireland may have been a greater dissuading influence.[8] Yet, Kathleen's religious pursuits were based in a deep spirituality, an embrace of nature and an unfailing compassion for the most vulnerable of humanity. Kathleen's was not an unquestioning allegiance to an institution. Instead, like

---

7 Emma Donoghue, *Passions Between Women, British Lesbian Culture 1668–1801* (London, 1993) p. 3.

8 Author interview, 9 May 2000.

many progressives of her time, she strove to live a concept of Christianity which eschewed power and supremacy and placed love and fellowship at the heart of its teaching. Kathleen was acutely aware of the need to reform the Church of Ireland to give it more relevance to its congregation and worked with those like Douglas Hyde to de-Anglicise the Church.[9] Her sense of spirituality and connection with early Celtic Christianity, laced as it was with so much of the old religion, was in keeping with her quest to be fully expressive of who she was without the constraints placed on her by virtue of gender and religion.

Kathleen was not alone amongst her suffragist contemporaries in establishing a lasting, committed political and domestic relationship with another woman. Louie Bennett and in later life Helena Molony also lived out their days with women partners. The most well-known lifelong partnership among Kathleen's female contemporaries was that between Eva Gore-Booth (sister of Constance Markievicz) and Esther Roper. This couple often moved in Kathleen's circle and her diaries make mention of times shared in their presence or correspondence exchanged.[10] Like the Gore-Booth/Roper partnership, Kathleen and Madeleine shared every important aspect of their lives in the company of women:

> It is . . . a misleading belief . . . that the term lesbian refers solely to a sexual practice and not to a mode of life in which a woman's political, intellectual, emotional, social and sexual energies are focussed on other women.[11]

Kathleen Lynn's home was always shared with other women and for most of her adult life with one woman, Madeleine ffrench-Mullen. It is clear that their life together was enriched by an extensive network of women friends, sister political activists,

---

9 Medb Ruane, 'Kathleen Lynn' in *Female Activists, Irish Women and Change 1900–1960*, Cullen and Luddy (eds) (Dublin, 2001).

10 Kathleen Lynn's Diaries: 24 June 1917, Kathleen accompanies Eva and Esther to Bodenstown; 21 October 1917, notes that she has sent a letter off to Eva.

11 Lesbian History Group, *Not a Passing Phase, Reclaiming Lesbians in History 1840–1985*, (London, 1989) pp. 77–98.

academics, artists and professionals from Ireland, Britain and the United States – many of whom where themselves in lifelong partnerships with other women. Yet, these realities are ignored or dismissed as insignificant or coincidental by heterosexual biographers and historians. It is my contention that these elements are conscious choices and are emphases made by Kathleen which constitute the fabric of a vibrant and determined lesbian approach to living and loving. I recognise the importance of those elements of her life because it mirrors so much of my own and that of my lesbian friends.

There is another assumption at the heart of the historical discourse that desexualises women's relationships with one another. That is, the conviction that women either (a) did not experience sexual impulses (a theory that defies the tide of nature); or (b) if they had experienced sexual impulses, would never have acted upon them because of the mores and proscriptions of the time. Yet, there is ample evidence that not only Kathleen but also many other women activists in history challenged convention to breach previously male-only territory. It is those acts of rebellion that have brought these women to our attention. These women did not ask for permission or allow the constraints of their sex to impinge upon their aspirations and self-expression. The absence of a language with which to express their sexual desire and to acknowledge their own sexual pleasure does not indicate an absence of sexual awareness, but only confirms the paucity of a female-centred discourse in relation to sexuality. As one noted lesbian historian has commented:

> One aspect of women's biography that deserves close attention is that of friendship. Patriarchal history decrees that the only woman worthy of notice is the one who has danced upon men's stage, to a script prepared and directed by men, in company with other men. In this perversion of history, men whose roles were really minor are allowed to dominate the stage while the vital female members of the cast are crowded off. . . The reality is that women have women friends and women lovers and that these are central not peripheral relationships however

> much society tells us that our lives should revolve around men.[12]

Despite their strong belief in the righteousness of their cause, feminist or nationalist, it is difficult to imagine how women such as Lynn and her contemporaries found the stamina and the courage to continue their struggles against such overwhelming odds. A reading of the texts and an analysis of the time and its politics[13] make clear, however, that all the women involved crossed and criss-crossed one another's paths time and again, providing a deep well of personal support and encouragement to draw upon. The official histories demonstrate this fact with the continual repetition of familiar activist names engaged in a multiplicity of organisations, movements or initiatives together. They were alliance builders, political comrades and co-activists. These women cannot but have known each other well, because the extent of their activities and involvements is much greater than their numbers would lead us to believe is possible. When primary and personal sources are accessed it is thus confirmed that their friendships were crucial and enhancing elements not only of their political lives but also of their emotional and social existences.

The improvement of women's social, economical and political position had particular attractions for women who did not wish to marry or be dependent upon men, not least of which was the camaraderie and joy of working closely with other convention-defying women. The intensity of the campaigning work involved and the pleasure to be derived from sharing time and space with like-minded women were aspects of suffrage and

---

12 Rosemary Auchmucty, 'By Their Friends We Shall Know Them: The Lives and Networks of Some Women in North Lambert 1880–1940' in Lesbian History Group (ed.), *Not A Passing Phase, Reclaiming Lesbians in History 1840–1985* (London, 1989) pp. 77–98.

13 Clíona Murphy, *The Women's Suffrage Movement and Irish Society in the Early Twentieth Century* (London, 1989); also Rosemary Cullen Owens, *Smashing Times: A History of the Irish Women's Suffrage Movement 1889–1922* (Dublin, 1984); Margaret Ward, *Unmanageable Revolutionaries: Women and Irish Nationalism* (Dublin, 1983).

social change movements which would have enhanced emotional commitments and strengthened intimacies amongst women. Indeed, for many women the presence of such an environment may have been as equally attractive as the ideology that gave rise to it.

The struggle for recognition of women's contribution to history and the continual need to hold the territory wrung from the academy has led many women historians to portray their female subjects as asexual. They have, as a result, chosen to subdue or sacrifice the sexual life or inclinations of their subjects to the objective of reclaiming their political agency. Perhaps the best example of the contortions to which biographers have stretched in denying a sexual life between women is in this extract from Gifford Lewis's biography of Eva Gore-Booth and Esther Roper:

> . . . but when we consider the sheer confidence in their mutual love of Eva and Esther, arranging to be buried in the same grave with a quotation from Sappho on their gravestone, there obviously was a socially acceptable route through companionate love – it was mystic, soulful and not physical.[14]

Here, Lewis has denied any sexual reading into their partnership. Yet, at the time of Eva's death in 1926 there was no confusion over who Sappho was or what Sapphism meant, and equally so in the late 1980s at the time of the Lewis biography. The passions stirred between women active in suffrage campaigns are particularly evident in the relationship between Eva Gore-Booth and Christabel Pankhurst. The end of this relationship impelled Eva to pen the following:

> The lamp has gone out in your eyes,
> The ashes are cold in your heart,
> Yet you smile indifferent-wise,
> Though I depart – though I depart.

14 Gifford Lewis, *Eva Gore-Booth and Esther Roper, A Biography* (London, 1988) p. 100.

Other verses read:

> I was the Force that made you strong
> From your brain to your finger tips,
> And lifted your heart in a song,
> And fashioned the words on your lips.
> I was the Hour that made you great
> I was the Deed you left undone,
> The soul of love – the heart of hate,
> I was the Cloud that hid the sun.[15]

As Lewis admits, these are poems of 'mourning and loss'. Christabel had quite publicly rejected Eva after an intense relationship between the two that was noted in Sylvia Pankhurst's autobiography as 'remarkable' for the change it wrought in Christabel's otherwise selfish and self-aggrandising character. Indeed, Sylvia remarks that Mrs Pankhurst, their mother, 'was intensely jealous of her daughter's new friendship' and 'complained . . . bitterly that Christabel was never at home now'.[16] At the time of the relationship, Christabel was in her early twenties and Eva was in her early thirties and living with Esther Roper.

Lewis is a little at a loss in explaining the passions released in the Christabel/Eva connection. She dispenses with Christabel's involvement as 'whatever form of love Christabel felt for Eva' and then retreats into the relatively familiar and conventional interpretation of Eva and Esther's coupledom to reassure her readers that their love was 'companionate'. The benign rationale behind the denial of the nature of these relationships is to have the subject made visible within mainstream historiography by accepting the hetero-patriarchal constraints of that recognition. It is hard, however, to rule out the probability of the biographer's own difficulties in acknowledging the true nature of such relationships.

Another dilemma faced by the feminist student is that of reading into historical intimacies between women conceptions

---

15 Eva Gore-Booth, 'The Body to the Soul' and 'The Soul to the Body', from *The One and the Many* (London, 1904).

16 Sylvia Pankhurst, *The Suffragette Movement* (London, 1977).

of sexuality that have been developed and defined in more contemporary times. Hence, definitions of lesbianism accepted by late twentieth-century society that place emphasis on sexual relations between women are not always appropriate when studying our historical foremothers. Yet, many female historical figures such as Gertrude Stein, Janet Flanner, Eleanor Roosevelt and Kate O'Brien do comply with these criteria. However, to achieve accuracy of sexual definition it is important to link it to periodization.[17]

It is important, therefore, to examine the social and cultural contexts in which women like Kathleen operated and particularly the way in which the politics of the New Woman was perceived both by radical women themselves and the establishment. Carroll Smith-Rosenberg[18] summarises the New Woman as white, middle or upper class, born between the late 1850s and early 1900s, educated, ambitious and most frequently single. By the early twentieth century, New Women had established places for themselves within the new professions. They had asserted their right to a public voice and visible power, and demanded rights and privileges customarily accorded only to white middle-class men. The presence of the New Woman challenged existing gender relations and the distribution of power. By insisting on her own social and sexual legitimacy, the New Woman repudiated the 'naturalness' of the bourgeois order.

In response, the establishment – in particular the medical profession – began to promote the construction of progressive women as 'unnatural'. Medical texts began to address the phenomenon of the New Woman, constructing her as deviant:

> The female who possessed of masculine ideas of independence, the virago who would sit in the public highways

17 Martha Vicinus, ' "They Wonder to Which Sex I Belong". The Historical Routes of Modern Lesbian Identity' in Denis Altman (ed.) *Which Homosexuality?* (London, 1989).

18 Carroll Smith-Rosenberg, 'Discourses of Sexuality and Subjectivity: The New Woman, 1870–1936', in Martin Dubermann *et al* (eds), *Hidden from History: Reclaiming the Gay and Lesbian Past* (London, 1989) pp. 264–280.

> and lift up her pseudo-virile voice, proclaiming her sole right to decide questions of war or religion or the value of celibacy and the curse of woman's impurity, and that disgusting anti-social being, the female sexual pervert, are simply different degrees of the same class-degenerates.[19]

Kathleen would not have been unaware of the perceptions and constructs which the sexologists and others would have placed upon her relationship with Madeleine. As a doctor she would have had access to many of the early twentieth-century medical debates on independent, feminist women and their relationships together. She would have been aware too of how those views were exercised to prevent women from achieving their political goals. In the United States, for example, a political campaign against feminist reforms was launched citing the sexologist Havelock Ellis as an unimpeachable expert.[20] Boarding schools and colleges that encouraged women's independence and sisterhood were particularly targeted. The New Woman was unable to respond to this quasi-medical sexual attack and her silence has been interpreted by Rosenberg as having its roots in the Victorian culture into which they were born:

> . . . in which sex in the absence of men was inconceivable. As a result having eschewed men sexually, they had no language in which to conceive of their erotic relations with other women as sexual; they could not construct themselves as sexual subjects.[21]

Without a language with which to describe and self-define women's sexual existence, any kind of related discourse was seriously proscribed. Writing in 1915, the feminist Stella Browne noted that:

> The realities of women's lives have been greatly obscured by the lack of any sexual vocabulary. While her brother

19 William Lee Howard, 'Effeminate Men and Masculine Women', in *New York Medical Journal*, No. 71 (1900) p. 687.

20 R W Schufeldt, 'Dr Havelock Ellis on Sexual Inversion', in *Pacific Medical Journal*, 65 (1902) pp. 199–207.

21 Smith-Rosenberg, p. 273.

> has often learned all the slang of the street before adolescence, the conventionally 'decently brought-up girl' of the upper and middle classes, has no terms to define many of her sensations and experiences.[22]

Yet, the absence of an obvious sexual language did not completely prevent women from finding other ways of articulating their intense feelings for one another or indeed the physical nature of those feelings. Some correspondents used allegorical references or masked their gender by taking on the personae of popular novels or even Biblical characters.[23] Others used code words shared only with their intimate to allude to feelings or activities that would otherwise have been deemed inaccessible or inappropriate for two women to experience. There is some evidence of this latter approach in Kathleen's diaries (see Chapter 2).

## Kathleen and Madeleine

Kathleen and Madeleine loved one another deeply and passionately. If they were alive today, I have no doubt that they would be called lesbians. They shared a home for almost three decades. They had fun together. They laughed and conspired. They missed each other desperately when apart and fretted over one another's perceived risk-taking. They rowed over finances, had people to dinner and took in women friends who needed shelter. They stole time together to be alone, collaborated on their grand project of St Ultan's, had 'perfect weekends' in Wicklow[24] and argued and made up like any other couple. No man ever made a dent in their commitment to one another or ever caused them to separate. In fact, no man was ever allowed to get that close.

22 Stella Browne, 'The Sexual Variety and Variability Among Women', cited in Sheila Robotham, *A New World of Women: Stella Browne – Socialist Feminist'* (London, 1977) pp. 104–105.

23 For examples of using characters from popular fiction or Biblical contexts to convey feelings in intimate correspondence between women, see Hart and Smith (eds), *Open Me Carefully, Emily Dickinson's Intimate Letters to Susan Huntingdon Dickinson* (Ashfield, Massachusetts, 1998).

24 Kathleen Lynn's Diaries, 4 December 1916.

In exploring the aspects of Kathleen's life that for personal reasons have interested me, I am deeply conscious of the injustice that I am doing to Madeleine. Madeleine exists here only because of her relationship to Kathleen and when she is seen it is through Kathleen's eyes. Despite the many loving and admiring references that Kathleen makes about her, there is much more that needs to be added to the portrait of the woman who was Madeleine ffrench-Mullen and who was so much more than Kathleen's partner. Her energy and vitality, inferred from many of the diary extracts and the doggedness with which she pursued ideas and campaigns, are evident from a reading of other historical texts. Speaking after Madeleine's death, one friend of Kathleen and Madeleine's comments on 'her marvelous way of overcoming insuperable things'.[25] Madeleine's fearlessness is described in Kathleen's diary when she is arrested for 'spying' by the Black and Tans during the War of Independence and again when Kathleen is arrested during the Civil War. Kathleen attributed her release to the fact that 'M. made a great fuss'. Moreover, if increased knowledge were available of Madeleine, the richness of the relationship between herself and Kathleen might be more fully appreciated. However, that relationship notwithstanding, a biography of Madeleine ffrench-Mullen, suffragist, children's columnist, freedom-fighter, Republican, Sinn Féin councillor, nurse and co-director of St Ultan's Hospital is long overdue.

The coyness with which relationships like that of Kathleen and Madeleine are still treated by historians is painful for someone like me to witness. By failing to acknowledge the depth and strength of women's commitment to one another and the span of their intimacies, it is not just the historical subjects who are diminished but those of us who love women today. By refusing to address the importance of homoeroticism between women historically, the implication is that contemporary lesbians are some kind of modern aberration with no foremothers, and most

25 17 October 1944, Kathleen's diary refers only to this friend as 'M'. Author believes it may have been Meg Connery, who knew both Kathleen and Madeleine well and who had served with them in 1916.

Plate 2: Kathleen Lynn and Madeleine ffrench-Mullen circa 1916.
*Courtesy of National Library of Ireland.*

callously of all, without a cultural past and without an historical contribution. In much the same way, the recent school of Irish historical revisionism attempted to negate and erase the progressive character of republicanism and its contribution to a legacy of political challenge in Ireland. Biographers, some of whom are feminist historians, have sought to justify their discomfort and embarrassment about lesbians in Irish history by desexualising and sanitising the biographies of their female subjects.

## WRITING WOMEN INTO IRISH HISTORY

History in Ireland has been an almost unchallenged male domain, with parameters and standards based upon the exclusivity of the male experience, perceptions and reading. Irish feminist scholars have fought to provide a wider lens through which history could be viewed, encompassing the role and experiences of the other half of society. Acceptance has not been easy, nor access to the 'old boys' academy readily given. Nevertheless, in recent years it has become harder to dispute the view of history which feminist research and analysis has provided. Women's past roles and lives have had to be unearthed and painstakingly restored to us. It has been an arduous task for feminism to gain mainstream recognition for this work, and that recognition is still grudgingly drip-fed. Perhaps the scars from these efforts have caused some feminist historians to shy away from addressing the woman-to-woman sexual and romantic connections of their subjects for fear of further vilification from their male colleagues. Perhaps the absence of such recognition also masks the biographers' own discomfort with female-to-female liaisons. Whatever the reason, in failing to acknowledge and celebrate the loving and intimate desires that existed between women they provide only a two-dimensional representation of those women's lives, perpetuating into the present the stigma that has concealed from us their subjects' most essential selves.

## My affinity with Kathleen

I make no secret of my penchant for Kathleen. Over the past few years, as I have become more intimately acquainted with her life, I have toyed with the notion that she is seducing me by offering a little of herself at a time; always just enough to keep me intrigued and anticipating her next revelation. Yet, I have a feeling that if we had been contemporaries – either in her time or here now in mine – we might have been wary of one another. We share commitment to Republican ideals, a dedication to women's empowerment, and a love of our own sex, but the class difference might well have put distance between us. Kathleen had a no-nonsense approach to her politics and projects, and her diaries exhibit a brusqueness that sometimes jars on modern sensibilities. She was no poet and, from the evidence, not an inspiring orator. My irreverence and Northern cynicism, my abhorrence of party rules, and my own capacity for bluntness (not to mention my weakness for eloquent orators) could prevent us from developing a closer friendship. Nevertheless, I know I would want her respect over that of many others and she would have easily won mine. I concede to being a little in love with Kathleen, because for such a long time as a Republican feminist who loves women I could find no reflection of myself amongst my contemporaries and the discovery of an historical predecessor ended an aloneness that I never willingly chose.

# Chapter 1

## EARLY LIFE

At first glance, Kathleen Florence Lynn would appear an unlikely candidate for revolutionary politics and even less so an espouser of a united Irish Socialist republic. Born on 28 January 1874 into the Protestant, Anglo-Irish middle classes, Kathleen's life pointed towards a comfortable, genteel, pro-Unionist future amongst the rural county set of Mayo, assisted by the patronage of the powerful Lord Ardilaun of Guinness renown.[1]

The family of Kathleen's mother, Katharine Wynne, was descended from the Earl of Hazelwood and was part of the landowning classes of Sligo-Leitrim. Kathleen's maternal grandfather was a clergyman, the Rev. Richard Wynne of Drumcliffe, Co. Sligo. Her father, Robert Lynn, was the son of a Sligo doctor and graduated in Divinity from Trinity College, Dublin. Medicine and religion were to remain central influences and motivations throughout Kathleen's life.[2]

Kathleen's birthplace of Mullafarry, near Kilalla in Co. Mayo, had lost two thirds of its population in only three decades and in 1874 was a struggling testament to the ravages of famines. The unrelenting poverty and the daily hardships of its people would have been evident to the young Kathleen as she accompanied her mother on various errands of mercy and almsgiving, tasks that befitted the wife of a Victorian clergyman.

---

1 Mullafarry (Ballysakerry) baptismal records, courtesy of Very Rev. Dean E.G. Ardis.

2 Hazel P. Smyth, 'Kathleen Lynn, M.D., FRCSI' in *Dublin Historical Record*, 30 (Dublin, 1977) pp. 51–57; Dr J.B. Lyons, *Brief Lives of Irish Doctors 1600–1965* (Dublin, 1978) p. 159.

In 1882, Kathleen, along with her three siblings, Annie Elisabeth (1873, known as Nan), Emily Muriel (1876) and John Willoughby (1877) moved with their parents to Shrule, Co. Longford, where the Rev. Lynn had been appointed as rector to the parish. Shrule was a little more affluent than North Mayo and the Rev. Lynn appears to have made impression enough to win the attention of the Ardilauns. In 1886 they offered him a living and, under their sponsorship, the facilities of a substantial rectory in Cong. One of the few personal musings on her early life available to historians quotes Kathleen as having been impressed by the work and ministrations of 'the local doctor', who 'was the font of help and hope and so I decided to become a doctor'.[3] Medb Ruane identifies the doctor as Kathleen's uncle, Dr Smartt of Shrule.[4] Ruane offers another formative incident: the young Kathleen, on overhearing a conversation among adults about the survival of a valuable piece of Waterford crystal throughout the 1798 rebellion, marvelled at how an object could excite such passion when so many human lives had perished.[5]

Cong would certainly have been the culmination of her parents' aspirations. The Guinness residence, Ashford Castle, was and still is a magnificent and opulent place. It was often the venue for the most prestigious events in the social calendar of the wealthy upper classes, with even royalty making an appearance. Affluent and salubrious as the Ardilaun estate may have been, this area of Mayo had been devastated by famine. It consequently had been the site of heated political activity generated by the Ladies' Land League, conditions and circumstances that would not have gone unnoticed by the young and impressionable Kathleen. Cong, however, would be a place that Kathleen would visit more often than reside in. A few years after the family's relocation there she would begin the education that would eventually lead to more than just a geographical distance from her family.

3 *Ibid.*

4 Author interview 9 May 2000.

5 *Ibid.*

## Alexandra College

Perhaps Alexandra College can take most credit for shaping and directing the young Kathleen's burgeoning social conscience and instilling in her a lifelong commitment to women's equality. Alexandra College, Dublin, was one of the first educational institutions for girls in Ireland. Its founder, Anne Jellicoe, had hoped to open a school for the training of governesses in 1866. She set out to model it on Queen's College, London, and to provide 'a liberal education in the best sense; a broad understanding of principles'.[6] However, neither Jellicoe nor Alexandra College were content to remain on the sidelines of the struggle for women's higher education, and the College was soon in the vanguard of the women's education movement. In the lobby for the Intermediate Education Act 1878, the success of Alexandra College was cited as evidence of the desire for secondary-level education for girls.[7] The Intermediate Education Act permitted girls to take public examination at secondary-level and was soon followed by the Royal University Ireland Act in 1879. Although the Act was primarily designed to provide alternative third-level access to Catholic males, it was also extended to women. Ironically, Trinity College, Kathleen's father's old alma mater, refused both Catholics and women. The Royal University Act provided an examining body at degree level and students chose their own college and enrolled for exams set by the RUI. At intermediate level a system of money prizes was awarded to the schools of the best students, and for many schools this was their main source of income. Unfortunately, with the arrival of the Catholic, Dominican-controlled St Mary's College for girls in Eccles Street, the awards system was sometimes the cause of competitiveness within girls' education. The Dominicans in Eccles Street took no small amount of triumphant pleasure if a St Mary's girl outstripped her contemporaries at Alexandra:

---

6 Anne V. O'Connor and Susan M. Parkes, *Gladly Learn and Gladly Teach: A History of Alexandra College and School, Dublin 1866–1966* (Dublin, 1984) p. 10.

7 Endowed Schools Commission, 1879–1880, p. 31 (cited at fn 6 above).

> We do not wish to make any ungenerous comparisons but at a time when it is not unusual to suggest that the convent schools are unequal to a programme of higher education, it cannot be uncalled for to state the fact that on this, the first occasion when the Alexandra College and a convent school came into open competition for the great prize in connection with the examination for the highest degree in the ARTS, the convent school remains the victor.[8]

By the time that Kathleen arrived at Alexandra in 1891 the curriculum and the interests of the college were rapidly expanding under the steady leadership of its Principal, Henrietta White. A number of the college's first graduates were already on the teaching staff. Hockey and a cycling club developed during Kathleen's years, as did the college magazine. Cycling was a mode of transport that Kathleen embraced for most of her life. Florence Culwick, a close friend of Kathleen's who remained steadfast throughout the most controversial period of Kathleen's political life in 1916, later became music teacher at Alexandra College. By the time that Kathleen took her RUI degree in 1895, Trinity University was still resisting entrance to women students. It would be 1902 before the hallowed gates of Ireland's first university would open to women and then only to enroll in arts degrees, with medicine available soon after.[9]

Alexandra College strove to imbue its students with both a sense of female solidarity and philanthropy. In 1897, the year that Kathleen's graduated from her medical studies, the Alexandra College Guild was established 'to form a bond of union among present students: to keep past students in touch with the College, to encourage the undertaking by them of useful work and to interest them in and inform them about women's work'.[10] The Guild encouraged good works and was responsible for a number of initiatives amongst Dublin's poor and

---

8 *Ibid.*, p. 64.

9 J.B. Lyons, 'Women in Medicine', *Irish Times*, special supplement, January 1992, pp. 38–40.

10 O'Connor and Parkes, *Gladly Learn and Gladly Teach* (Dublin, 1984) p. 69.

working classes. Patrons, as well as students past and present, were associated with the Guild, and a number of Kathleen's contemporaries and past acquaintances had links to the organisation. In 1898, Dr Katharine Maguire, who had graduated in medicine a few years earlier than Kathleen and later served on the Board of St Ultan's, presented a paper to the Guild entitled 'Social Conditions of Dublin's Poor'. This lecture appears to have galvanised Guild members into social action, culminating in a tenement housing scheme. The Lynn family patroness, Lady Ardilaun, provided the resources for an emergency fund for the relief of the Guild's tenants during times of unexpected hardship brought about by illness and unemployment.[11] Given Kathleen's lifetime work among the poor of Dublin and the career she followed, the Guild would have been an important contact and network for both her professional endeavours and her early philanthropic activities.

Graduates of Alexander College were to forge careers in many non-traditional areas, such as medicine, law and journalism. It has been argued that the greater numbers of Protestant women in education and entering the professions may have been in some part related to the absence of ecclesiastical constraints experienced by their Catholic counterparts.[12] Another factor was that Protestant middle-class dominance of commercial and other interests at that time would have substantially increased employment opportunities for graduates from colleges such as Alexandra.

Alexandra College was more than a pioneering institution with regard to advancing the cause of women's education in Ireland. It also laid strong foundations of solidarity and sisterhood amongst its student body and staff, encouraging independent thought and social action. Anna Haslam, founder of the Irish Women's Suffrage and Local Government Association (IWSLGA), was a regular visitor to the college, and throughout the life of the IWSLGA many Alexandra staff and former pupils

---

11 *Ibid.*

12 Maryann Valiulis, in address to Royal Irish Academy on 8 December 1999.

were registered members. Women's suffrage was therefore an underpinning theme within the curriculum, and the socio-economic status of its student body fitted the profile of that movement: educated, middle class and Protestant. A further example of Alexandra's liberal approach to education is the introduction of Irish-language classes to the curriculum in 1904. Entitled 'Celtic', these were taught by Padraic Pearse, a later acquaintance and comrade of Kathleen's.

Legislation introduced in 1876 allowed medical bodies to grant qualifications 'to all persons without distinction of sex'.[13] The medical profession was a difficult and entrenched body which was not sympathetic to the arrival of women in its midst. It took some time before there were breaches in the wall of disapproval. The Royal College of Surgeons in Ireland (RCSI) included women in their classes from 1885 and the Catholic University School of Medicine in Cecilia Street, Dublin, admitted female students in 1896.[14] Kathleen took classes in both. She was awarded degrees in medicine, surgery and obstetrics from the Royal University in 1899, having interned at Holles Street Hospital (1897–99), the Rotunda Hospital (1899), the Royal Victoria Eye and Ear Hospital (RVEEH) in the same year, and the Richmond Lunatic Asylum.[15] She was refused a post of resident doctor with the Adelaide Hospital in 1898 on the grounds that the hospital had no suitable female residence, but she did obtain the first female residency at the RVEEH.[16] To further soften the blow of her rejection by the Adelaide, Kathleen won the Barker Anatomical Prize from the Royal College of Surgeons. In December of that year the Alexandra College magazine congratulated her 'recent successes as one of the most gifted women student doctors'.[17] She also provided consultancies at other hospitals, including Sir

13 F.O.C. Meenan, *Cecilia Street: The Catholic University of Medicine 1855–1931* (London, 1987) pp. 83–95.

14 *Ibid.*

15 Medb Ruane, forthcoming.

16 *Ibid.*

17 Kathleen Lynn's Records courtesy of Mary O'Doherty, Mercer Library, Royal College of Surgeons in Ireland.

Patrick Dun's. In 1904 she made her home in 9 Belgrave Road, Rathmines, from where she operated her general practice and lived for the rest of her life.

# Chapter 2

## Women's Activism in Ireland 1900–1916

A Quaker couple, Anna and Thomas Haslam, established the first Irish women's suffrage association in 1876, which eventually became known as the Irish Women's Suffrage and Local Government Association (IWSLGA).[1] The IWSLGA was the training ground for many women activists who would later be prominent in both the suffrage and the nationalist movements. The first acknowledgement of Kathleen's involvement appears in the subscribers' list of 1903. By 1905, she is a member of the National Committee along with her peers Hanna Sheehy Skeffington and Jenny Wyse Powers.[2] The former would be a founder of the Irish Women's Franchise League in 1908 and the latter a member of Sinn Féin, becoming its Vice President in 1911.[3] Kathleen maintained her membership of the IWSLGA until 1917.

The centenary of the 1798 United Irishmen Rebellion reawakened nationalist sentiments in many parts of Ireland and sections of Irish society. It heralded a renaissance in all things Gaelic: language, sports, history and music. For many of the emerging political activists of the coming decades, these interests and related activities were the springboard to the founding of a new nationalist movement. The Gaelic League offered

1 Rosemary Cullen Owens, *Smashing Times: A History of the Irish Women's Suffrage Movement 1889–1922* (Dublin, 1984) pp. 23–25.

2 Annual reports and subscriptions lists of Irish Women's Suffrage and Local Government Association 1900–1917, National Library of Ireland, 3996 i3.

3 R. P. Davis, *Arthur Griffith and Non-Violent Sinn Féin* (Dundalk, 1974) Appendix 1.

activities that were open to both men and women alike, despite the disapproval of the Catholic establishment, which preached against the 'obscenity' of young men and women dancing together at ceilidhes.[4] The Gaelic Revival, whilst endorsing an often romanticised ideal of the Gael, nurtured the belief that the continued influence of perfidious Albion was the main obstacle preventing the Gaelic spirit from flourishing.

Queen Victoria's visit to Dublin in 1900 galvanised the indomitable Maud Gonne[5] into action. With a number of other women, she organised the Patriotic Children's Treat Committee for those children who did not take part in the Royal celebration.[6] This Ladies' Committee was so successful that it decided to retain its collective agency and Inghinidhe na hÉireann was born. Inghinidhe was the first nationalist women's organisation to be formed since the Ladies' Land League had been forced to disband in 1882. It was a response to the exclusion of women from other nationalist organisations.[7] Inghinidhe became so popular – organising children's classes in Irish and, as a protest against British influence, supporting Irish produce and promoting Irish writing and drama – that in 1908 it launched its own paper, *Bean na hÉireann*.[8] Abbey actress Helena Molony was its first editor, contributors also included journalist Sydney Gifford, writing under the pen name of 'John Brennan', Constance Markievicz, providing a sometimes rather gruesome gardening column, poet Katherine Tynan and

4 P.T. Mac Ginley, 'The Irish Language Movement and the Gaelic Soul', in W. Fitzgerald (ed.), *The Voice of Ireland* (Dublin and London, 1924) p. 450.

5 Maud Gonne, the daughter of a British Army officer, was a prominent and active supporter of the Land League. She was well regarded by Arthur Griffith and other male nationalist leaders, and she used her charm and legendary beauty to open doors that would otherwise have been closed to her as a woman.

6 Margaret Ward, *Unmanageable Revolutionaries: Women and Irish Nationalism* (Dublin, 1983) pp. 47–50.

7 Ruth Taillon, *When History Was Made: The Women of 1916* (Belfast, 1996) p 1.

8 *Bean na hÉireann*, vol 1 No. 6–25 and vol. 2 nos. 23–24, National Library of Ireland, IR 3996 b15 and IR 05 p. 15.

Madeleine ffrench-Mullen. Although it is not known if Kathleen was a 'signed-up' member of Inghinidhe, there is some suggestion that she was a fellow-traveller. The following letter to *Bean na hÉireann* in 1909 bears all the hallmarks of Kathleen, the doctor with a social conscience and a contempt for establishment hypocrisy:

> As a person who takes a great interest in any scheme run by a person for the amelioration of Ireland I should like to ask Lady Aberdeen, through the medium of your paper to favour me with a few statistics concerning her tuberculosis crusade: that, if supplied, would no doubt, be a great aid to others wishing to help in the same cause. One of the most important things to study would be the effect of certain work and certain diet on the Irish constitution, and this can best be done by taking one class and examining the statistics procurable concerning them.
>
> Would Lady Aberdeen supply us with the number of Bishops (Catholic and Protestant), Priests, Protestant Clergymen and Ministers of the various Nonconformist Sects and curates of all denominations who, during the last five years, have been under treatment for consumption?
>
> I am sure that the publication of those facts would be a great asset in the hands of those engaged in the tuberculosis campaign.
>
> Yours truly,
>
> *KATHLEEN*[9]

The Lady Aberdeen referred to in the letter was Vice-Reine of Ireland, wife of the British Lord Lieutenant and Vice-Regal of Ireland. Lady Aberdeen incurred the wrath of Inghinidhe for her arrogance in purporting to represent the women of Ireland, 'The Lady Lieutenant can represent nothing in Ireland but English officialdom'.[10] The paper very much reflected Inghinidhe's militant nationalism and opposition to constitutionalist reform – whether through Home Rule or the introduction of women's

9 *Ibid.*, Vol. 1 No. 7, 1909, National Library of Ireland, IR 3996 b15.

10 *Ibid.*, Vol. 1 No. 8, 1909.

Plate 3: Inghinidhe na hEireann (1905–1906). Maude Gonne is seated in the centre holding the group's banner. Unfortunately it has not been possible to identify the other group members all of whom wear Inghinidhe's badge based on the Tara brooch. *Courtesy of Kilmainham Gaol and Museum.*

suffrage – arguing that both required recognition of British sovereignty over Ireland. Kathleen's tone in the letter shows she too had no love for the British administration in Ireland, and thus shares the sentiments of the paper and its founding organisation. A possible contact with Inghinidhe may have developed through her friendships with members Jenny Wyse Power and Ella Young, who like Kathleen were activists within the IWSLGA.

Around the same time as *Bean na hÉireann's* appearance in1908, Inghinidhe, Clann na nGaedhael (an umbrella grouping of Gaelic clubs) and the Dungannon Clubs (an Irish Republican Brotherhood front) combined to form Sinn Féin.[11] The

11 Ward, *Unmanageable Revolutionaries*, pp. 66–67.

organisation was pledged to work peacefully through Irish institutions for Irish independence. Several women were elected onto its Executive Committee, among them Jenny Wyse Power. Many Republican separatists – including Helena Molony and Mary MacSwiney[12] – refused to join, however, because Arthur Griffith, its President, had a particularly archaic view of Irish independence, involving a dual monarchy for Ireland and Britain. After 1916, when Sinn Féin became the dominant, organised voice of Irish Republicanism, Kathleen too would become a key activist and a member of its Executive Committee, or Ard Comhairle.[13]

The struggle for women's suffrage was also intensifying. Anna Haslam's IWSLGA, with its genteel and reformist outlook, began to frustrate a new younger breed of women who were no longer prepared to wait for piecemeal reforms and wanted change through direct action. Hanna Sheehy Skeffington and Gretta Cousins, both protégées of Anna Haslam, broke away from the mother organisation, with Haslam's acceptance if not blessing, to form the militant suffrage organisation, the Irish Women's Franchise League (IWFL).[14] The IWFL was to become the most outspoken and public manifestation of women's discontent and radical feminism in Ireland. Its journal, the *Irish Citizen*, provided an important propaganda tool and ideological discussion forum on all the emerging political issues of the day.[15] The IWFL and its paper critiqued national and international political developments from its own pacifist, internationalist and feminist standpoint. The primary aim of the IWFL was to secure women's suffrage within the promised Home Rule Bill, the political platform pursued by Redmond's Irish Parliamentary Party.

Tensions existed between nationalist feminism's prioritising of Ireland's independence first and foremost and the IWFL's open

---

12 Mary MacSwiney was to become President of Cumann na mBan in Cork, and took an active role in preparations for the 1916 Easter Rising in Cork city and county. She was elected to the First Dáil and was a leader of a 31-day hunger strike by women Republican prisoners during the Civil War.

13 See Chapter 3.

14 See Margaret Ward, *Hanna Sheehy Skeffington, A Life* (Cork, 1997) for a detailed history of the founding of the Irish Women's Franchise League.

15 *The Irish Citizen 1912–1920*, National Library of Ireland, POS 8882.

skepticism about pinning women's progress onto some nationalistic ideal of a new Ireland. Despite heated arguments that often erupted on the pages of the *Irish Citizen* and on public platforms, there was collaboration between the two movements. In 1910, nationalist feminists and some militant suffragettes worked together to bring about the extension of the School Meals Act to Ireland. Again in 1913 they were to be found shoulder-to-shoulder in supporting the families and the cause of labour during the Dublin Lock-Out.[16]

By 1913 increasing anxieties about Unionist militancy in the North and Carson's armed Ulster Volunteer Force, pledged to resist any form of Home Rule, led to the formation of the Irish Volunteers. At its inaugural meeting over half of the 6,000-strong audience joined up. Many nationalist women attended this meeting, but were confined to a 'ladies' gallery'.[17] This was an indication of the way in which women were to be viewed by the new movement. Inghinidhe had shown that women could match men in militant nationalism and now that an openly militant organisation committed to defending independence by force of arms had been established, women's exclusion from it became a bitter pill to swallow. Controversially, it was decided to establish a women's auxiliary organisation in support of the Volunteers. One hundred women attended Cumann na mBan's (Council of Women) first meeting on 2 April 1914, where the following aims were adopted:

1. To advance the cause of Irish liberty;
2. To organise Irishwomen in furtherance of this object;
3. To assist in arming and equipping a body of Irishmen for the defence of Ireland;
4. To form a fund for these purposes to be called the 'Defence of Ireland Fund'.[18]

---

16 Ward, *Unmanageable Revolutionaries*, pp. 80–83.

17 *Ibid.*, Chapter 3, 'Cumann na mBan, 1914–1916, The Early Years', pp. 88–118.

18 Cited in Margaret Ward, *In Their Own Voice, Women and Irish Nationalism* (Dublin, 1995) p. 44.

Inghinidhe merged with Cumann na mBan the following month, but retained its own identity as a separate branch. If tensions were often obvious between the suffragettes and Inghinidhe, those between the IWFL and Cumann na mBan were even more marked, despite both organisations sharing a strategy in campaigning for the introduction of Home Rule. Hanna Sheehy Skeffington was scathing of Cumann na mBan, believing them to have set back the women's agenda by establishing a subordinate organisation to the Volunteers rather than making a direct challenge to the exclusion of women.[19] She regarded Cumann na mBan as women who had been duped into becoming 'a collecting box' for the men.

Ironically, hostility between women's organisations affiliated to Republicanism and equal rights feminists has prevailed into the late twentieth century in Ireland. Disputes between the two currents were particularly acrimonious throughout the 1970s and 1980s in the North. Liberal feminists characterised Republican feminists as pawns of a patriarchal movement and accused them of being divisive. Republican women, in turn, insisted that demands for Irish women's equality must be linked to challenges to the sectarian inequalities faced by Catholic women in the North. They argued that equality could never be realised within the sectarian, Unionist-dominated Northern Ireland state.

After 1916, Constance Markievicz became Cumann na mBan's President, urging its members on to ever more strenuous and daring activities. Kathleen Lynn provided Cumann na mBan members with first-aid training, as she also did later for the Irish Citizen Army in Liberty Hall.[20] Unlike her friend the Countess, however, Kathleen never joined Cumann na mBan. Her close friendships with many of its members do not appear to have influenced her to join, and one can only surmise that her own perception of Cumann na mBan was of an organisation that could not fulfil her aspirations for equality and primacy of action.

The Dublin Lock-Out of 1913 left its mark on many women activists, several of whom found a more supportive and

19 *The Irish Citizen*, 17 April 1915.

20 Ward, *Unmanageable Revolutionaries*, p. 103.

conducive home for both their feminist and nationalist beliefs in James Connolly's Irish Citizen Army (ICA).[21] ICA women had equal status to male members. Kathleen Lynn, Madeleine ffrench-Mullen, Helena Molony and Constance Markievicz were all officers trained and equipped on a par with their male counterparts. They, in turn, retained lifelong commitments to the cause of labour and the emancipation of the working class. Hanna Sheehy Skeffington and her husband Frank were also members of Connolly's Socialist Party of Ireland. Their pacificism prevented involvement with any form of militarism, however.[22] Although not affiliated to an armed organisation, Hanna did deliver food to rebel garrisons during the Easter Rising.[23] Helena Molony, with Louie Bennett and Helen Chenevix of the Irish Women's Suffrage Federation, invested a significant part of their political lives building the Irish Women's Worker Union (IWWU), inspired by the labour politics of Connolly. Kathleen was a staunch supporter of the IWWU. When the union re-organised in the aftermath of 1916, Kathleen and Madeleine ffrench-Mullen were both elected to the position of Vice-President.[24]

During this period some individuals, including Kathleen, fostered relationships across the movements, but only two were able to provide consistent bridges. Constance Markievicz was involved in any initiative that advanced the cause of freedom for the Irish, whether man, woman or child. Her alliances and involvements were sometimes propelled more by exuberance than analysis; nevertheless she gained the respect of all and still remains the most enduring female historical figure to emerge from that period. Yet, it was James Connolly more than any other individual who provided the unifying ideological framework for feminism and nationalism: setting both within the Marxist theory of class and labour, he produced the most progressive of ideologies, Irish Republican socialism.

---

21 Donal Nevin, 'The Irish Citizen Army, 1913–1916' in Donal Nevin (ed.), *James Larkin: Lion of the Fold* (Dublin, 1998).

22 Ward, *Hanna Sheehy Skeffington*, p. 135.

23 Taillon, *op. cit.*, p. 68.

24 Mary Jones, *These Obstreperous Lassies: A History of the Irish Women Workers Union 1889–1922* (Dublin, 1984) p. 46.

Plate 4: Members of the Irish Women Workers Union who took part in Easter 1916. *Courtesy of National Library of Ireland.*

This then was the radical stew that the newly graduated Doctor Kathleen Lynn would have encountered in Dublin at the start of the twentieth century. But when and at what point did she enter this maelstrom of activity? There are a number of possible access points through which the young graduate of Alexandra College and the female pioneer of Irish medicine might have initiated contact with these networks of activist women.

As a member of the IWSLGA, Kathleen would have been acquainted with Hanna Sheehy Skeffington and Greta Cousins. It is known that she was a member of IWFL at least in the latter years of that organisation's existence.[25] Alexandra College was an enthusiastic patron of the Irish language, although Irish was not introduced to the school curriculum until after Kathleen's graduation. The school's interests and those of its past pupils

25 Cullen Owens, *Smashing Times*, p. 119.

often coalesced. Perhaps Kathleen became involved in one of the many Gaelic organisations that sprang up around the turn of the century. Both Helena Molony and Constance Markievicz became close friends of Kathleen, and Molony is given credit for introducing the Countess to her first Inghinidhe meeting; perhaps she performed similar introductions for Kathleen.[26]

In 1912, at a mass meeting of suffragists attended by all the Irish suffrage organisations to demand the inclusion of female suffrage in the Home Rule Bill, Kathleen was one of those present on the platform.[27] Certainly by 1913, Kathleen was well known to both militant suffragettes and nationalist feminists. She replaced Dr Elizabeth Tennant as Hanna Sheehy Skeffington's doctor after Tennant was found to be too inexperienced in dealing with prison authorities during one of Hanna's imprisonments for suffrage activism.[28] Ruane and Cullen Owens have her assisting in 'the soup kitchen with Delia Larkin, Hanna Sheehy Skeffington, Helena Molony, Madeleine ffrench-Mullen and Constance Markievicz' during the Lock Out of the same year.[29] As a result of this involvement she was invited by Connolly to join the ICA.[30]

There is, however, one other connecting thread that links the nationalism and feminism that were to become central tenets of Kathleen's life, and that is Madeleine ffrench-Mullen, Kathleen's lifelong partner. Madeleine was a member of Inghinidhe na hÉireann, writing a children's column for their paper *Bean na hÉireann* and other articles under the pen names of 'Dectora' and 'M. O'Callaghan'.[31] She also engaged enthusiastically with the campaign to introduce school meals to Dublin children and staffed Liberty Hall's soup kitchen throughout the 1913 Lock Out. By 1914, both Madeleine and Kathleen, along with the Countess, Helena Molony and Nellie Gifford, are officers in the Irish Citizen Army operating out of Liberty Hall. Kathleen's

26 Ward, *Unmanageable Revolutionaries*, p. 68.
27 Cullen Owens, *Smashing Times*, p. 51.
28 Ward, *Hanna Sheehy Skeffington*, p. 120.
29 Medb Ruane, *Ten Dublin Women* (Dublin, 1991) p. 62.
30 *Ibid.*
31 Sydney Gifford, *The Years Flew By* (Dublin, 1974) pp. 48–53.

relationship with Madeleine is one that requires examination, for not only did they closely mirror each other's politics, but they also established a partnership that went beyond a shared political ideology and extended to every aspect of their lives.

## Kathleen and Madeleine

Kathleen's early diaries are kept during the most difficult and turbulent years of Ireland's history, when clandestine and subversive activity was at its height. One can easily understand how Kathleen would feel the need to use either circumspect language or coded references when alluding to persons or activities which, if discovered, could have had severe consequences for all involved. However, there is one particular diary entry where there is obvious usage of a code word but without any political or military reference involved. The unfamiliar word would appear to be of German origin and is used in the following entry: 'M (Madeleine) *grussed* me as the clock struck last night.'[32]

This entry is made on Kathleen's birthday, 28 January 1921. Grüssen is the German word for greet and that language would have been familiar to both Kathleen and Madeleine as each had spent time living and studying in Germany. It seems most unlikely that this was a simple greeting between two friends – for why else would Kathleen disguise the activity? There is undoubtedly something special about this 'greeting' because it takes place on the eve of Kathleen's birthday and requires a special word, a covert word to distinguish it from the usual form of greeting.

Madeleine was her closest political ally, her sister-officer in the ICA, her confidante, her partner in the great life-consuming project of St Ultan's. She was also her financial adviser, for there is evidence in the diaries that Kathleen hated anything to do with accounts and taxes.[33] Kathleen and Madeleine were more than a good working team; they were dynamically effective and inexorably bound to one another.

---

32 Kathleen Lynn's Diaries, 28 January 1921.

33 Kathleen Lynn's Diaries, 21 November 1923 and 4–5 December 1923. These extracts detail Kathleen's hatred of tax collectors and accountants,

There is no reason to suppose that the nature of their relationship was unknown to friends and comrades. Rosamund Jacob, a member of the IWFL and of Cumann na mBan (referred to in the diaries as Roisin Jacobs[34]), wrote a novel in the 1920s (not published until 1938) entitled *The Troubled House*.[35] The novel is set during the War of Independence and involves the various roles taken by members of the fictional Cullen family. One of the themes explored is the sacrifice of a woman's identity, the mother, to that of the men in her family. This is juxtaposed with the more independent lives of two characters, Josephine and Nix, who are described by Jacob's biographer, Damian Doyle as a 'strongly suggested lesbian relationship of two artists'.[36] Interestingly, these lesbian characters provide refuge to an IRA character and are consequently raided and their artwork destroyed. The presence of Republican-minded lesbians would appear to have been strong enough and recognisable enough to have warranted inclusion in a novel of the times.

But it is in recording their most private times together and her feelings of being apart from Madeleine that Kathleen's diaries depart from their usual brusqueness and provide insights into the profoundly loving nature of their relationship. A trip to Glencormac together is described as the 'most perfect weekend'.[37] After an absence caused by Madeleine's treatment for a goitre the diaries note, 'M. coming home to me to-morrow'[38]; and 'Madeleine home, made front room nice and cosy'[39]; 'M. and I had nice private breakfast'[40]; '. . . It is very lonely in No. 9 without Madeleine'.[41]

---

describing St Ultan's auditors' offices as 'the fortress of the jeykells [sic]' 31 January 1923.

34 *Ibid.*, 31 December 1922.

35 Rosamund Jacob, *The Troubled House* (Dublin 1938).

36 Damian Doyle, 'Rosamund Jacob' in *Female Activists, Irish Women and Change 1900–1960.*

37 *Ibid.*, 26 November 1916.

38 *Ibid.*, 4 December 1916.

39 *Ibid.*, 5 December 1916.

40 *Ibid.*, 9 March 1919.

41 *Ibid.*, 4 March 1921.

Should there be doubt about the depth of her relationship with Madeleine, one particular excerpt from her diaries should dispel it. Written after Kathleen was transferred from the overcrowded conditions of Kilmainham Gaol – where she and Madeleine had shared a cell with several other women – to the relative comfort of Mountjoy Prison, the entry conveys the intensity of her feelings: 'Mountjoy clean and comfortable, but I'd give £10,000 for Kilmainham and Madeleine'.[42]

The entries relating to Madeleine's death are amongst the most moving. Madeleine died on 26 May 1944 after a long illness. Kathleen was 70 at the time of her death and their partnership together had lasted 30 years:

> . . . a beautiful day, got some wee flowers from the garden & a bunch of yellow roses & went & said goodbye to the earthly MffM & sat there a while in the stillness, the yellow roses make the coffin so sweet.
>
> . . . crowds at Whitefriar St. All knew me & not the family. My hand was tired shaking.[43]
>
> . . . the loneliness (of) coming back, with no MffM to greet me & say what a barren wilderness it had been while I was away.[44]
>
> So so lonely for dearest MffM.[45]
>
> To-day more than ever I realise that M. is gone.[46]

Kathleen chose to make her home in Rathmines at Belgrave Road, a thoroughfare populated by other feminists.[47] In all of her political endeavours she lost no opportunity to challenge established responses to women and her belief in women's

42 *Ibid.*, 10 May 1916.

43 *Ibid.*, 28 May 1944.

44 *Ibid.*, 5 June 1944.

45 *Ibid.*, 6 June 1944.

46 *Ibid.*, 26 June 1944.

47 Margaret Ward, *Hannah Sheehy Skeffington*, p. 222. Ward lists amongst its residents Hanna Sheehy Skeffington and her sometime lodger Rosamund Jacob, Kathleen and Madeleine and their regular lodger Helena Molony, and next door to them fellow Republicans Una and Robert Brennan, Sinn Féin's director of publicity in 1918–19.

equality ran in parallel to her other political involvements. As a physician she was on close terms with many women, including Hanna Sheehy Skeffington, Kathleen Clarke, Constance Markievicz, Helena Molony and Mary Hayden. In her mid-forties she combined her medical and feminist commitments by establishing St Ultan's Hospital as an exclusively women-run institution, introducing practices and techniques of healthcare pioneered by other women, such as Maria Montessori and Drs Dorothy Stopford Price and Patricia Alston.[48]

It is clear that at every opportunity over which she had control, Kathleen actively sought out or created women-centred environments in which to live, work and pursue her beliefs and ambitions.

Recent research by Professor Martin Pugh indicates that lesbianism, far from being a fringe element within British suffragism, was an active sexual choice of many of its leaders. The diary of a close confidante of British suffragettes the Pankhursts, details with candour the various couplings of Christabel and Emmeline Pankhurst with other activists, such as Annie Kenny and Ethel Smyth.[49] The moral and social constraints on these women were no less or greater than those placed on Kathleen and her contemporaries in Ireland. If the genteel daughter of a Unionist clergyman could take up arms in the cause of Irish nationalism and find justification for her actions, might she not also live contentedly with a more private rebellion against the sexual mores and expectations of her gender?

---

48 Medb Ruane, *Ten Dublin Women*, p. 65.

49 'Diary reveals lesbian love trysts of suffragette leaders' in *The Observer* 11 June 2000. The article reports the discovery by Professor Pugh of the personal diary of WSPU activist Mary Blathwayt, who Pugh believes was the lover, for a brief time, of Christabel Pankhurst, 'before she was supplanted in Christabel's affections by Annie Kenney'.

# Chapter 3

## Kathleen Lynn's Easter Rising 1916

> We watched the little bodies of men and women march off – Pearse and Connolly to the GPO, Sean Connolly to the City Hall. I went with the Doctor in her car. We carried a huge store of first aid necessities and drove off through the quiet, dusty streets and across the river, reaching the City Hall just at the very moment Commandant Sean Connolly and his little troop of men and women swung around the corner and he raised his gun and shot the policeman who barred his way. A wild excitement ensued, people running from every side to see what was up. The Doctor got out, and I remember Mrs. Barrett – sister of Sean Connolly – and others helping to carry in the Doctor's bundle. I did not meet Dr Lynn again until my release, when her car met me, and she welcomed me to her house where she cared for me and fed me up and looked after me till I had recovered from the evil effects of the English prison system.[1]

Most accounts of the 1916 rebellion have Kathleen stationed at Dublin's City Hall throughout the action of Easter Monday, 24 April. Several other ICA women, including Madeleine, were stationed at St Stephen's Green. Ruth Taillon's account of City Hall and the activities of Dr Lynn are most detailed and rely on accounts from Matt Connolly, brother of Sean, and Jenny Shanahan, who was also stationed at City Hall.[2]

---

1 Constance de Markievicz, *Cumann na mBan Journal*, Vol. 11, No. 10, Easter, 1926, National Library of Ireland.

2 Ruth Taillon, *When History Was Made, The Women of 1916* (Belfast, 1996) pp. 53–56.

Sean Connolly's objective was to take Dublin Castle but a policeman barred the way, and Connolly shot him, as described in Markievicz's account above. He ordered his force to go in but a moment's hesitation meant that the gates were closed to them. Helena Molony fired a shot at the soldier responsible and another comrade hurled a bomb at the guardroom; but the bomb failed to explode and the attempt seemed doomed. Connolly decided that the advantage of surprise had been lost and ordered his small troop to take their positions in the adjacent City Hall and the *Evening Mail* offices on the other side of Dame Street. From these vantage points ICA sharpshooters could pin down the garrison at Dublin Castle. The rebels were well prepared for the siege at City Hall, having previously had copies of the keys of the building made.[3] Connolly's force was comprised of 16 men and nine women, among them the Norgrove sisters, Emily and Annie, Molly O'Reilly, Jenny Shanahan, Helena Molony, Katie Barrett (Sean Connolly's sister), Brigid Davis and Kathleen Lynn.[4]

Sean Connolly was wounded early in the afternoon of Easter Monday as he raised the tricolour over City Hall. By the time Kathleen crawled across the rooftop under fire to administer aid to him, he was dead, with his head cradled in Helena Molony's lap. Sean Connolly's death left Kathleen, a lieutenant in the ICA, as senior officer in charge of the outpost. Despite their vantage points, the small force, now without their commandant, came under heavy fire from the Castle. Helena Molony and Molly O'Reilly went to the GPO to ask for reinforcements but there were none to be had. City Hall and the *Evening Mail* offices were assailed by heavy machine guns. Later that same evening Kathleen sent for Sean Connolly's 15-year-old brother, Matt; she told him of his brother's death and the sterling nursing work being done by his sister Kate. Kathleen examined the young Matt and ordered him to get some sleep, relieving him from his post as sniper on the rooftop of

---

3 Connor Kostick & Lorcan Collins, *The Easter Rising: A Guide to Dublin in 1916* (Dublin, 2000) p. 116.

4 Taillon, *When History Was Made*, pp. 53–56.

Plate 5: Some of the women who took part in the Easter Rising. Photo taken in Ely O'Carroll's garden, 1916. Kathleen and Madeleine are seated on the ground in front row to right and left. *Courtesy of Kilmainham Gaol and Museum.*

City Hall. It would appear that Kathleen's motive for this action was to prevent the death of another young man from the same family. Certainly, it did save Matt Connolly's life. Matt Connolly's memory of that night was awakening to find that, 'the building seemed to shudder and vibrate with explosions and machine gun fire. Glass crashed, doors and woodwork were being shattered, and somewhere in the distant part of the building a woman screamed.'[5]

Kathleen's diaries begin on Easter Monday 1916. Her description of events is short, even abrupt: 'Easter Mon. Revolution. Emer [Helena Molony] and I in City Hall Seaghan [sic] Connolly shot quite early in day.'[6] It is likely that Kathleen made this entry after the events in City Hall. It may have been

5 *Ibid.*

6 Diaries, 24 April 1916. This is the first entry in Kathleen's diaries.

shock and secrecy that kept her account so brief, but one also detects the stoicism of the physician speaking.

After the capture of their outpost the women, among them the Norgrove sisters, Katie Barrett and Brigid Davis, were taken to Ship Street barracks, close to Dublin Castle. Kathleen wrote, '. . . we were locked up in a filthy store, given blankets thick with lice and fleas to cover us and some "biscuits" to lie on, not enough to go round'.[7] Another account of the 'store' where the women were kept recounts that it contained offensive-smelling rubbish bins that Dr Lynn insisted should be removed. As a physician she was aware that such debris and offal could cause serious risks to health.[8] There is some irony in this, given that the women had not only risked their health but put their lives in imminent danger for almost 24 hours before.

This sense of outrage at the conditions to which the prisoners were subjected has a particular basis in Republican rationale. Throughout the entire events of the Rising and the preparations beforehand, there was an adherence to military protocols of war and battle amongst the rebels and they followed an honour code. Macardle writes that The O'Rahilly, charged with finding a means of escape from the GPO, first assured himself of the safety of the 13 British prisoners that the rebel HQ had taken. Then, in an effort to advance scout a route out through Moore Street, he was shot dead.[9] The story of the Stephen's Green park keeper coming twice a day to feed the ducks, and combatants preserving a ceasefire to allow him to do so, has lost none of its pathos;[10] nor has that of Pearse surrendering his sword at the post in Parnell Street to Brigadier-General Lowe.

These stories capture the underlying sense, perhaps misplaced or even profoundly foolish, that both sides in a war subscribe to a belief in the essential nobility of the combatants. Kathleen, a woman notably succinct, took twice as long to recount the state of her prison quarters as she did to describe

---

7 *Ibid.*

8 R. M. Fox, *The Green Banners: The Story of the Irish Struggle* (London, 1938) p. 153.

9 Dorothy Macardle, *The Irish Republic* (London, 1937) p. 164.

10 Kostick & Collins, *The Easter Rising*, p. 78.

Plate 6: Aftermath of shelling in Henry Street, Dublin, Easter 1916. Nelson's Column on O'Connell Street can be seen in the background. *Courtesy of National Library of Ireland.*

the traumatic events that preceded her captivity or even those that followed. This is an indication of her shock that her captors did not respect the honour code she expected to underpin the treatment of a surrendered foe.

Kathleen was held in Ship Street Barracks from 24 April to 1 May. The surrender of the rebels came on Saturday, 29 April, and was couriered to all remaining insurgent outposts by Elisabeth O'Farrell, who soon joined Kathleen in Ship Street.[11] The centre of Dublin lay in ruins; 142 British soldiers and policemen, 64 Volunteers and an estimated 254 civilians had been

11 Interestingly, Elisabeth O' Farrell is buried in the National Grave Plot in Glasnevin. She died in 1957 and is buried with her 'faithful comrade and lifelong friend, Sheila Grenan'. The gravestone was erected in 1961. (Information supplied by Irish National Graves Association.)

killed, and a further 2,000 wounded. Dublin's Fire Brigade Chief put the cost of damaged buildings at £1.1 million, with almost £1 million of stock lost.[12]

On 1 May Kathleen, like the majority of republicans arrested, was moved to Kilmainham Gaol.[13] The Gaol had been taken over as an army detention barracks at the start of the First World War, originally having operated as a convict prison until 1910. By the time the Republican prisoners arrived, the gaol was without heat or light because the gas supply had been cut off by the Irish Volunteers during the fighting. The women were held in the older west wing, built in the 1790s and in serious disrepair with very poor sanitary facilities.[14] Despite the conditions and the frightening uncertainty as to her eventual fate, Kathleen wrote on 2 May: 'Saw MffM (Madeleine ffrench-Mullen) early this mg. Greatest joy.'[15] Yet again, Lynn's brevity would belie the emotional content of the situation. The depth of her love for Madeleine and the affection between them would have made the intervening days and events until their reunion unbearable. The anxiety of not knowing where Madeleine was or even if she was alive are characteristically reduced to the simple but profound response of, 'Greatest joy'.

Kathleen, Madeleine and Helena Molony shared a cell together and consequently the conditions of her imprisonment were made more tolerable with the company of her most intimate friends. Constance Markievicz was kept in solitary confinement and allowed no contact with the others. Unknown to most of the women prisoners, the surviving male leaders of the Rising were also held in Kilmainham. As the executions took place the truth began to dawn: 'On Tues. Wed. Thurs. at 3am we heard volleys fired under cell windows. On Tues. 3, Wed 3, Thurs 1. We hear they have shot members of the Provisional Govt.' 'Heard 3 shots this mg. Told later on Mallin, Ceannt & Colbert had been shot'.[16]

12 *Ibid.*, p. 125.

13 Kathleen Lynn's Diaries, 1 May 1916.

14 Sinéad McCoole, *Guns & Chiffon: Women Revolutionaries and Kilmainham Gaol*, (Dublin, 1997) pp. 29–30.

15 Kathleen Lynn's Diaries, 2 May 1916.

16 *Ibid.*, 3–8 May 1916.

Lt.-General Sir John Maxwell, commander of the British Forces in Ireland, decided who should be detained further and allocated the prisoners to their eventual places of confinement. Many of the women were released, their sex a deciding factor in their fate. On the evening of 8 May, the women in Kilmainham were ordered to the central hall. Those whose names were called had to cross to one side and were informed of their release.[17] Twelve women, known to the police before the Rising, were further detained. Despite Maxwell's distaste for imprisoning women, he believed it would be unwise to have these women 'at large'. Among them were Countess Markievicz, Helena Molony, Madeleine ffrench-Mullen and Dr Kathleen Lynn.

On 10 May, Kathleen was moved to Mountjoy Gaol.[18] Kathleen's diary entries from this period cease one week later, on 17 May. During the first week of June, Kathleen's beloved Madeleine was released, along with four of her comrades. The remaining women were transported to England. Kathleen's family had influential contacts and strong representations were made to prevent her from being incarcerated in an English prison. They argued for Kathleen to be taken into care with a family friend, the rationale being that she was '. . . a sort of lunatic', as Kathleen later recalled.[19] Naturally, Kathleen rejected such interventions but the Great War had placed onerous demands on medical practitioners and physicians were urgently needed in England. With the help of Jenny Wyse Power, who took no part in the Rising, work was arranged for Kathleen with Dr Cusack, a Galway man working as a locum at Abingdon outside Bath. In July of that year, her sister Muriel was taken ill and permission was granted for Kathleen to return to Cong to minister to her. By the time she returned in August to Dr Cusack's practice the authorities had agreed she could

---

17 McCoole, *Guns and Chiffon*, p. 31.

18 Kathleen Lynn's Diaries, 10 May 1916.

19 Kathleen Lynn's statements to the Military History Tribunal. Lynn's Home Office 1916 files have been destroyed (D.R. Taylor, Home Office, to Ruane, 19 February 1996). See correspondence between Home Office, Dublin Castle and Dublin Metropolitan Police, National Archives of Ireland, 13503/6.

return to Dublin.[20] Two of the women internees were released in July and the other three the following December. Constance Markievicz, who had been sentenced to life imprisonment, was released in June 1917.

Kathleen Lynn is described as 'the sole female doctor with nationalist sympathies'.[21] Just how did these sympathies develop to the stage where she jeopardised her professional and personal relationships by joining a revolutionary army and taking part in an armed uprising? Kathleen has left no intimate reflections on her involvement, nor any explanation of her motivations. In the absence of such material, a new lens must be taken to the personal records of the diaries.

In the week before her deportation, Kathleen's family and family friends commenced a concerted campaign to persuade her to disavow her comrades and her politics. The diary entries show how difficult this time was for Kathleen. These are the only sustained comments on her emotional responses to her situation and the first insights into the rift with her family. The day before her transfer to Mountjoy, she notes that a message was delivered to her from family friends, the Carletons, advising her 'to give up her Republican friends'.[22] The following day her father, 'Fardie', comes to remonstrate with her in Mountjoy and the visit is obviously a distressing one for both: '. . . it is hard to grieve one's father, but I could not do otherwise.'[23]

On 12 May, the family renew their assault. Both her sister and father visit her with disturbing effect:

> A very black Friday. Fardie and Nan were here, oh so reproachful, they wouldn't listen to me and looked as if they would cast me off forever. How sorry I am for their sorrow! Erin needs very big sacrifices. I am glad they go home to-morrow. Why do they always misunderstand me?[24]

20 NAI, 13503/16.
21 Ward, *Unmanageable Revolutionaries*, p. 103.
22 Kathleen Lynn's Diaries, 9 May 1916.
23 *Ibid.*, 10 May 1916.
24 *Ibid.*, 12 May 1916.

There is a poignancy to this entry. It is the voice of a daughter, a sibling whose actions have confounded and shamed her family, and she is bewildered by their reaction. Kathleen's final sentence implies that her troubles with the family are not new ones; the question does not appear to be rhetorical. Rather, it is a plea for understanding and enlightenment as to how she has become so dislocated from them. Some days later she writes, 'Saw D. Maguire yesterday and Dora Carleton, both very disapproving. Lizzie Smartt today the same'.[25] These are Kathleen's peers in background and social position. Kathleen had betrayed the expectations of her gender, her social class, the politics of that class, her family and her profession. She had sacrificed all that for a bloody, ill-fated armed rebellion, allying herself with people whom her family and their friends looked upon as a bunch of rebels and renegades. It is not difficult to understand the frustration and anger of her family and old friends. But how does one understand Kathleen?

Kathleen's mother Katharine died in 1915; her anniversary is noted regularly in the diaries and frequent trips to her grave in Deansgrange cemetery are recorded. After Katharine's death, Kathleen was closest to her mother's unmarried sister Florence. It was in the Dun Laoghaire home of dear 'aunt Flo' that Kathleen found unquestioning acceptance and perhaps something like the maternal love that she so missed. Kathleen is buried with Katharine Wynne, in the grave that Kathleen and Flo visited often together and where flowers were always laid.[26] It was to Flo that Kathleen turned for solace and acceptance, particularly during the years after her involvement in the Easter Rising, when she was barred from the family home in Cong. Kathleen's despair and anguish over the estrangement is most palpable in the diaries at Christmastime. Despite the sisterhood and company of women friends and comrades throughout the year, the traditional season of family and hearth was a painful reminder of her loss, Aunt Flo's open door notwithstanding: 'Christmas with Aunt F. a happy day, tho' lonely, they won't

25 *Ibid.*, 17 May 1916.

26 Deansgrange Cemetery Plot No. 100/R.S./S.W.

have me still at home'[27] and '. . . when shall I go home again for Christmas?'.[28]

Finally, in 1920, the family relented at the eleventh hour (one wonders had Aunt Flo a hand in persuading them), but stringent conditions were attached to her visit: 'Letter by this mgs [morning's] post to say I may go home for Xmas if I won't have a demonstration (do they picture bands?), or see people not their visitors. I'll go joyfully but come back Mon.'[29]

Kathleen can return, but only as a demure daughter, and there is to be no radical talk or presence in the family home. With this kind of censorship – in the midst of a reign of terror by Black and Tans, arrests, deprivations and sanctioned killings, and Kathleen herself in the preceding year having to flee raids and go 'on the run' on occasions – it is unsurprising to learn that, despite Kathleen's best intentions, the visit was fraught. Her father preached a sermon on St Stephen's Day denouncing nationalists and justifying the actions taken against them. Not satisfied to insist his daughter submit to his will whilst in his home, he then willfully and publicly provoked her: '. . . Evening sermon annoyed me much, hate my father to be unfair. He should say nothing if he can only think of police'.[30] Despite her obvious desire to be accepted into the family and her efforts to comply with their conditions, Kathleen's was not a prodigal return to the fold. She took a stand against the family's condemnation of her beliefs, precipitating a row before her departure: 'We had argument re murders etc. before I left. I hope they take it as it was meant, for they only see one side. . .'[31]; 'they' being not only her father but also her two sisters Muriel and Nan. Muriel was a staunch Unionist and after Independence took up residence in Northern Ireland, stating her preference for living under the Union Jack.[32] The family had tested her desire to be with them and it appears that this

27 Kathleen Lynn's Diaries, 25 December 1917.
28 *Ibid.*, 16 December 1918.
29 *Ibid.*, 24 December 1920.
30 *Ibid.*, 26 December 1920.
31 *Ibid.*, 27 December 1920.
32 Author interview, 9 May 2000.

may have been anticipated, at least by Madeleine. The same entry ends, '. . . M [Madeleine] met me, she and I are glad I'm back.'[33] One can surmise the discussions between them before Kathleen returned to Cong and Madeleine's anxieties for her whilst there. The two often travelled separately on political business around the country or on errands for St Ultan's. It was unusual for Madeleine to meet Kathleen's train and it indicates the concern she must have felt for Kathleen's emotional well-being whilst at Cong. It is also interesting to note that Madeleine never accompanied Kathleen on any of her trips to the Lynn family home.

Robert Lynn died in 1923 and Kathleen was with him at the end.[34] It is not known if there had been a reconciliation between the two, given her determination to have her family accept her as she was. A tentative, perhaps conditional, arrangement seems to have allowed her to remain in contact, including infrequent visits to Cong up until the time of her father's death. The effort to remain in touch with her family seems to have emanated solely from Kathleen and required the sublimation of her own sensibilities as the price of their toleration. After 'Fardie's' death, Kathleen's unmarried sisters had to vacate the rectory for the next incumbent. The diaries indicate that Kathleen was keen to have them live close to her in Dublin. She made several efforts to find them appropriate accommodation, which were rejected.[35]

An interesting postscript to the Lynn family dynamics is the disappearance – after their mother's death – of Kathleen's younger and only brother, John. In the same year of her father's death, 1923, a diary entry on 3 November reads: 'John's birthday. Where is he to-day? I think off [sic] when I first heard of his birth, dear John.'[36] Ruane's research has uncovered that John, without taking leave of the family, had gone with his wife to Australia, later deserting her there whilst she was pregnant with a third child. In later years, Kathleen tracked down this

33 Kathleen Lynn's Diaries, 27 December 1920.

34 *Ibid.*, 8 April 1923.

35 *Ibid.*, April-May 1923.

36 *Ibid.*, 3 November 1923.

family and established contact with her only nieces and nephew.[37]

Kathleen's decision to become a doctor and the commitment it required – at a time when women were barred from many professions and their education still regarded as something of an aberration – indicates a profound motivation. Her strong sense of social justice led her to dedicate her skills to the service of the most disadvantaged, but in particular to the most vulnerable of all, the children. We can only speculate as to whether childhood experiences of vulnerability within her own family were at the root of her passionate empathy for her young patients.[38] Kathleen exerted herself far beyond most of her medical peers in her efforts to provide a more holistic approach to the physical and emotional needs of her charges. When she introduced Dr Maria Montessori and her methods to St Ultan's in 1934, Montessori had been denounced by the Vatican for her promotion of children's emotional and sexual consciousness. Ruane has pointed out that 'Both doctors shared a profound belief in the essential human and civil rights of the child'.[39] Kathleen was on a quest. It was not enough to save infants and children from the diseases and illnesses caused by poverty and neglect, nor to prevent the occurrence of such diseases by introducing the pioneering vaccination treatment of Drs Stopford-Price and Alston. Kathleen viewed children as individuals with rights and emotional needs.[40]

This was her life's work as a physician, a vocation developed in early childhood. There is little more than brief factual material on Kathleen's early life, most of it relating to the genealogy of her parentage and her father's professional progress. Neither was Kathleen given to introspection or much personal reflection in her own writings. She was a woman who acted, who identified an injustice in need of redress and took both personal and political steps to ensure its eradication. Even in this most

37 Author interview, 9 May 2000.

38 Interview with Ruane, where Kathleen's father's authoritarianism was discussed, 9 May 2000.

39 Ruane, *Ten Dublin Women*, p. 66.

40 *Ibid.*, p. 65.

basic of instincts, she differed from her family and siblings. It would appear from the few reminiscences left to us by Kathleen that her perceptions of conditions around her and her responses to them were at variance with those of her family from an early age. Kathleen, like many of the new generation of medical women, put her skills at the service of those most in need, but she went further than any of her contemporaries. Having witnessed grave social inequities, Kathleen was impelled to take direct action to overthrow the system she held responsible.

# Chapter 4

## Sinn Féin, Irish Republicanism and Kathleen Lynn

Sinn Féin was formed in 1908 and was inspired not so much by an ideology as by the idiosyncrasy of its founder, Arthur Griffith. His policy of a 'Dual Monarchy', one for Ireland and one for Britain, found little endorsement amongst nationalist activists. Nevertheless, in the pre-1916 broad church of nationalism, Sinn Féin was a believer in the doctrine of Irish independence.

With the formation of the Irish Volunteers in 1913, Griffith signed up; but ironically, given Sinn Féin's later historical profile, his endorsement of the Volunteer movement was qualified by his distrust of physical force methods.[1] It was not long before the Irish Volunteers experienced an organizational split, led by Redmond, leader of the constitutional Irish Parliamentary Party at Westminster. Redmond mistakenly believed that if Irish Volunteers fought in Britain's war against Germany, Home Rule would be more speedily served. Those Volunteers who opposed Redmond's leadership were dubbed 'Sinn Féin Volunteers' or 'Sinn Féiners' by the press.[2] Those who opposed Redmond were the most committed adherents of armed resistance to Britain's rule in Ireland and their views would eventually dominate Sinn Féin.

Griffith took no part in the 1916 Rising. Yet it was in the aftermath of this event that Sinn Féin became the rallying point for the surviving combatants and the resurgence of nationalist feeling that claimed Ireland. Whereas nationalist sentiment had been largely silenced by the onset of the Great War, after the

1 Macardle, *The Irish Republic*, p. 92.

2 *Ibid.*, p. 125.

Easter Rising there was a sea-change in public attitudes. This was due to a number of factors. England's treatment of the surrendered insurgents, the executions of the rebel leaders, imprisonments and deportations even of those not directly involved helped to turn the tide of public opinion from hostility to sympathy. The postponement of Home Rule, increasing fears of conscription in Ireland in order to fill the trenches of France, and the murmurings of Lloyd George's partitionist solution had caused shudders in Ireland, giving new impetus to the nationalist agenda. Despite the deaths and imprisonment of the core membership of militant nationalism, Britain succeeded in recruiting for the Republican cause more effectively than its proponents had done prior to 1916. Consequently, Sinn Féin became the name ascribed to a body of opinion rather than the reflection of an organised political party.[3] Amongst that body of opinion Kathleen's own views were not out of place.

In 1917, the remnants of the Irish Volunteers and Sinn Féin supported the candidacy of Count Plunkett of the nationalist Liberty Clubs in the Roscommon by-election. Plunkett won the Roscommon seat and called a Convention of Republicans in the April of that year. Although the various elements of the movement had co-operated in getting Plunkett elected, the tensions between respective ideologies were becoming more fractious. The aim of the Convention was to create one overarching political movement to press forward the agenda of establishing Irish independence. Those women, like Kathleen Lynn and her contemporaries in the ICA, Cumann na mBan and Inghinidhe, had continued throughout the preceding year to keep the spirit of 1916 alive. They had concentrated their energies on supporting the prisoners and their dependants, organising welcome ceremonies for the released, and ensuring that the memories of the executed leaders were kept vibrant through Masses and memorial events. The women demonstrated unswerving commitment to the Republican cause. Indeed, it was women who were largely responsible for the survival and reorganization of the nationalist movement in the period of repression that followed the

3 *Ibid.*, p. 125.

Rising. Despite this, they found that their male compatriots needed to be vigorously reminded of the promise made in the 1916 Proclamation of the Republic, of equal rights and opportunities for all the citizens of the future Republic.

## The League of Women Delegates/Cumann na dTeachtaire[4]

Plunkett's Convention in April 1917 established a Steering Committee of nine people to negotiate and prepare the basis for political reorganisation. It became known as the 'Council of Nine'; the only woman amongst its membership was Josephine Mary Plunkett, wife of Count Plunkett. Such obvious tokenism alarmed many women activists, who recognised that the convergence of Republican organisations into a single party was a pivotal moment in which to cement their place within Republicanism and to reestablish commitment to equal citizenship rights for women in a future Irish Republic.

The dissidents called a meeting in the home of Countess Plunkett to discuss the situation. Among them were representatives of Inghinidhe, Cumann na mBan, the Irish Women Workers' Union and women from the ICA, including Kathleen Lynn. This was the first meeting of a recognisable group of feminist nationalists convening to examine and promote their own interests within the Republican framework of activity. They agreed to meet regularly to examine political developments, but most importantly they were forming a caucus to promote the representation and participation of women in the reorganisation of Sinn Féin.

In June, the women met again to discuss with some urgency the news that six more members of the Steering Committee were about to be co-opted from amongst the recently released prisoners and none of these would be women. The meeting also learned that Countess Plunkett was unable through illness to participate in the next meeting of the Committee, now calling

4 Margaret Ward, 'The League of Women Delegates' in *History Ireland*, Autumn 1996, pp. 37–41.

itself the Sinn Féin Executive. They decided to appoint their own substitute, Dr Kathleen Lynn, to take her place. Kathleen was duly entrusted to bring the following resolution to the Committee's attention:

> Taking into consideration the number of members of your executive, we, representing the various interests of the great bulk of the women of Ireland, propose a representation of six, to be chosen by your body.'[5]

Apparently, this resolution was defeated or, more likely, ignored. The women continued to meet with increasing anxiety about their exclusion from critical political developments. At its next meeting, in July 1917, the Sinn Féin Executive did co-opt Constance Markievicz, recently released from Aylesbury Prison. Markievicz's involvement notwithstanding, the women still had serious difficulties in getting heard, much less represented within the new organisation. A letter naming their six representatives was sent to Sinn Féin; the nominees were Kathleen Clarke, Áine Ceannt, Kathleen Lynn, Jenny Wyse Power (who had been a vice-president of Sinn Féin under Griffith), Helena Molony and Alice Ginnell. This request was also refused. Further letters were sent, resolutions drawn up and there was even a deputation sent to the Sinn Féin offices. Finally, after four months of constant lobbying, they managed to extract a concession permitting four of their number to the Executive on condition that they all become members of Sinn Féin branches. One of the four was Kathleen Lynn.

A Sinn Féin Convention was looming at which the constitution of the reorganised party and its future programme and politics would be decided. At a meeting on 16 October the women's caucus Gaelicised their name to Cumann na dTeachtaire and drew up their own constitution with the following aims:

- To safeguard the political rights of Irishwomen;
- To ensure adequate representation for them in the Republican Government;

5 Minute Book of Cumann na dTeachtaire: Sheehy Skeffington Collection, National Library of Ireland, MS 21, 194.

- To urge and facilitate the appointment of women to Public Boards throughout the country;
- To educate Irishwomen in the rights and duties of citizenship.[6]

At the Sinn Féin Convention that same month, the following resolution previously prepared by Cumann na dTeachtaire was moved by Kathleen Lynn:

> Whereas according to the Republican Proclamation which guarantees 'religious and civil liberty, equal rights and equal opportunities to all its citizens', women are equally eligible with men as members of branches, members of the governing body and officers of both local and governing bodies, be it resolved: that the equality of men and women in this organisation be emphasised in all speeches and leaflets.[7]

Kathleen's speech in support of the motion is a conflicting mixture of her inherent no-nonsense, blunt style and an uncharacteristic, but most likely necessary, appeal to the paternalism of her male compatriots:

> Women and men are complements one of the other . . . as a whole I think that women are honster [sic] than men and work straight for their end without being held back by personal considerations. We see all around us a system rotten with corruption and intrigue. If women have their place it will be much easier to keep it honest and open and straight. There would have been no Easter Week had it not been for the women who urged the men to take action boldly. We have no doubt that Easter Week saved Ireland . . . We are inexperienced, different, timid, we ask the men with centuries of experience to give us a little help and encouragement at the start, so as to give us a fair share in the great work before us.[8]

6 *Ibid.*
7 Sinn Féin Convention Report, National Library of Ireland, MS 21, 523.
8 *Ibid.*

There is no evidence in either her political or medical career to show that Kathleen ever demonstrated timidity or inexperience in accomplishing what she wanted to achieve. Indeed, her reference to the honesty of women and their ability to work towards their ends 'without being held back by personal considerations' is one of the most directly autobiographical statements that Kathleen has left to posterity. In any event, the motion was passed by a majority of delegates.

Cumann na dTeachtaire's success was welcomed by suffragists throughout Ireland. The organisation's constitution actively promoted co-operation and joint activity with other women's organisations:

> Whenever it can be accomplished without sacrifice of principle because they are convinced that the bringing together of all Irishwomen to discuss matters of common interest on a neutral platform could not but be beneficial to all parties.[9]

The cause of Republicanism was gaining strength and coherence, but the place of women within the new party of Sinn Féin would demand constant vigilance and struggle. At the same convention where Cumann na dTeachtaire won their resolution, Éamon de Valera was voted in as President of Sinn Féin. The nationalist feminist struggle to take and maintain political territory within Republicanism would require the support of women from across the spectrum of women's organisations and platforms (and for generations to come). Their next battle was to hold the ground just taken and the challenge came all too soon.

## 1918 and the General Election

The newly formed 24-person Executive elected at the Sinn Féin Convention of October 1917 now included Constance Markievicz, Kathleen Clarke, Grace Gifford and Dr Kathleen Lynn. Grace Gifford's presence was almost certainly in homage

9 Sheehy Skeffington Collection, National Library of Ireland, MS 21, 194.

to her executed husband Joseph Plunkett, son of Count Plunkett. Although Grace, like her sisters Muriel and Sydney, was active in Republican and feminist circles, she is noted primarily for her work as an artist. The formidable Kathleen Clarke, also a widow of one of the executed heroes, was critical of Grace for playing little part in the politics of the Executive.[10]

Sinn Féin's popularity caused increasing concern and discomfort to the British. The almost wholesale rejection of conscription by Labour, Republicans and many suffragists had resulted in the inclusion of a clause making provision for 'people of Irish birth' to be regarded as of 'hostile origin' within the Defence of the Realm Act.[11] A further opportunity to restrict and suppress Sinn Féin personnel and their activities was the 'uncovering' of a purported 'German Plot' involving Sinn Féin.[12] A flimsy but convenient sequence of events, the 'Plot' was used as a means to justify wholesale arrests of Republicans. Kathleen's diaries throw some light on the scale of the repression, 'Heard that whole Executive are to be arrested',[13] 'Almost whole Executive arrested and deported. Myself "on the run" ',[14] 'German Plot "discovered" [sic] by French.'[15]

Field Marshal French had recently been appointed Lord Lieutenant-General and Governor General of Ireland, and it is clear from the emphasis used in the latter diary entry that Kathleen regards the 'German Plot' as his concoction. Kathleen was rescued from certain imprisonment after her arrest and detention at Arbour Hill Barracks when her deportation order was cancelled through the intercessions of Dublin's Lord Mayor. Influenza had reached epidemic proportions in the city and her services as a physician were urgently required.[16] Kathleen's female comrades on the Executive, Constance Markievicz and

10 Kathleen Clarke, *Revolutionary Woman: Kathleen Clarke 1878–1972. An Autobiography*, Helen Litton (ed.), (Dublin, 1991).

11 Cited in Macardle, *The Irish Republic*, p. 236.

12 *Ibid.*

13 Kathleen Lynn's Diaries, 17 May 1918.

14 *Ibid.*, 18 May 1918.

15 *Ibid.*, 19 May 1918.

16 *Ibid.*, 31 October 1918.

Kathleen Clarke, were not so fortunate. They were arrested along with Maude Gonne and sent to Holloway prison, where Hanna Sheehy Skeffington soon joined them.[17]

Despite the hardships to which Kathleen and her sister Sinn Féiners were subjected, they were nonetheless heartened by an event of great significance for women. The extension of the franchise through the Representation of the People Act in 1918 gave the vote to women over 30 and men of 21 years. It was still a long way from parity, for as Cullen Owens points out, 'This age provision avoided the immediate establishment of a female majority in the electorate'.[18] Limited though it was, the women's vote would prove instrumental in the forthcoming General Election.

The Sinn Féin election manifesto promised to withdraw Irish representation from the British Parliament and establish an Irish constituent assembly to reassert the principles of the Proclamation of Easter 1916.[19] Ireland was under military rule and the press was censored. Sinn Féin was banned as an organisation and over 100 of its core activists and leaders imprisoned. A Republican victory was crucial, as in reality this election was tantamount to a national plebiscite on Irish independence.

Perhaps, faith in the commitment to the resolution they had wrung from Sinn Féin at the previous year's Convention led nationalist feminists to believe that they would be automatically considered as candidates in the forthcoming election. But nothing was to come easily or automatically for women. It was not only the political mainstream that was resistant to sharing power with women. Only two female candidates were selected to stand for Sinn Féin: Constance Markievicz (still imprisoned in Holloway) to contest the St Patrick's Division of Dublin and Winifred Carney to an unwinnable seat in Belfast.[20] Sinn Féin's election machine provided little if any assistance to the women candidates, despite that organisation's open wooing of the

17 Ward, *Hanna Sheehy Skeffington*, p. 215.

18 Cullen Owens, *Smashing Times*, p. 126.

19 Macardle, *The Irish Republic*, p. 224.

20 Ward, "The League of Women Delegates and Sinn Féin 1917", *History Ireland*, Vol. 4, No. 3 Autumn 1996.

women's vote to secure election and its dependence on women activists to carry out the drudgery of electioneering work for its candidates.[21] The blatant neglect of women candidates did not go unremarked by either the candidates or their supporters. Winifred Carney wrote:

> I was disappointed losing the £150 in my case, which would with workers on the day of the poll have been recovered. I had neither personation agents, committee rooms, canvassers or vehicles, and as these are the chief features in an election, it was amazing to me to find that 395 people went to the ballot on their own initiative, without any persuasion. The organisation in Belfast could have been better – much better.[22]

The failure to put even a semblance of an election support strategy in place for Markievicz drew the wrath of feminists:

> The very nerve of Sinn Féin sets my teeth on edge. The one woman they have thrown as a sop to the women of the country has her interest neglected . . .[23]

Hanna Sheehy Skeffington complained about the shambles that prevailed in the St Patrick's constituency, where Markievicz was candidate, as 'the worst managed constituency in Dublin', and declared:

> As a woman's organisation we feel we have a duty in this matter and think it is a disgrace to the women's organisation if Madame Markievicz is let down by an inefficient committee.[24]

---

21 *Ibid.*

22 Winifred Carney to Joe McGrath, 10 and 24 January 1919, quoted in *In Their Own Voice, Women and Irish Nationalism.* Meg Connery to Hanna Sheehy-Skeffington, *Sheehy-Skeffington Papers* MS 22,684. National Library of Ireland.

23 Meg Connery to Hanna Sheehy Skeffington, *Sheehy Skeffington Papers* MS 22,684, National Library of Ireland.

24 Hanna Sheehy Skeffington to Nancy Wyse Power, 1919, *Sheehy Skeffington Papers* MS 24,091, National Library of Ireland.

It was therefore left to the suffrage and Republican women who had so much invested in these elections to provide a ready if inexperienced band of election workers. They did not let Constance down. Election day was 14 December. Kathleen wrote, 'A glorious sunrise and a lovely day, memorable for Ireland. We all hope. May our women's vote be used for good'.[25] The result was an overwhelming landslide for Sinn Féin and the election of the first woman parliamentarian in these islands, Countess Constance de Markievicz.

These years of frenzied activity to cement Sinn Féin and women's place within the movement appear to have been the beginnings of a turning point in Kathleen's political career. Despite the ensuing years of intensifying military conflict with Britain and the catastrophe of Civil War, which demanded her continued commitment and sacrifice, and at times placed her in personal danger, the events of 1917 and 1918 can be seen as preparing Kathleen's departure from the political frontline. The concerted efforts of Kathleen and her counterparts to get the recognition they deserved within Sinn Féin, only to have their case for representation undermined yet again, and the lack of support shown for women candidates must have dented her confidence in the brave new Republican vision.

New priorities were now emerging for Kathleen. Once admitted to the Sinn Féin Executive, she was appointed their Director of Public Health, an acknowledgement of her expertise on the state of health provision for Ireland's most disadvantaged citizens.[26] The influenza epidemic that kept her from deportation and imprisonment inflamed her concerns for the most vulnerable of Dublin's poor, the children. Kathleen's diaries, particularly in the latter months of 1918 and throughout 1919, are almost totally dominated by her exertions to vaccinate the city's populace.

The year of 1919 started well for Republicans, with the opening of the First Dáil Éireann. Kathleen's diary states,'Dáil

---

25 Kathleen Lynn's Diaries, 14 December 1918.

26 L.M. McCraith, 'Irishwomen and their Vote', *New Ireland Review*, 30 cited in Cullen Owens, *Smashing Times*, p. 118.

Plate 7. Constance Markievicz addressing Sinn Féin supporters, Kilkenny, 1917. *Courtesy of National Library of Ireland.*

Éireann. It was all it should be, simple, solemn, impressive – a great voice, God grant a continuance to the end.'[27] But already Kathleen was forging ahead with her plans to open a hospital for children with infectious diseases. She was also concerned about sexually transmitted diseases. Cumann na dTeachtaire in 1918 had hosted a conference of women's societies, calling on Irishwomen doctors and nurses to attend to discuss 'the serious menace of venereal disease in Dublin'.[28] The numbers of British soldiers in the city and their connection to the spread of syphilis provided the chance to score yet another point against British rule. It galvanised Kathleen and her sister compatriots into raising the issue across the suffrage movement with a new cry that 'British rule was affecting the health of the nation!'[29] Venereal disease was a scourge amongst Dublin's poor and, as Dr Margaret O'hÓgartaigh has pointed out, until Kathleen opened St Ultan's there was no policy for the treatment of children with

27 Kathleen Lynn's Diaries, 21 January 1919.

28 Cullen Owens, *Smashing Times*, p. 122.

29 *Ibid.*

syphilis.[30] Paediatrics, especially the treatment of children with infectious diseases, was a newly developing field of medicine. It had little of the status assigned to other medical specialities, being more closely associated to public health, a field that Kathleen did take seriously both as a doctor and a Republican.

The founding of St Ultan's Hospital in 1919 and its continual development, were to become a consuming passion for Kathleen for almost 40 years until her death in 1955.[31] While it is not the focus of this work, it would be an unforgivable omission to let its existence and the ground-breaking contribution its founder made to children's welfare and well-being in Ireland pass without notice. It would not have happened at all without the immeasurable determination, stamina and commitment of both Kathleen and her lifelong partner Madeleine ffrench-Mullen. Both were assisted in the hospital's early days by many of the most politically active women of the time, including Maud Gonne, Helena Molony, Kathleen Clarke, Charlotte Despard, Louie Bennett and Constance Markievicz.[32] The enormity of the challenge they shouldered is summed up in the remark of a male friend who, on visiting the site of St Ultan's quipped: 'If they were men, I'd say they were mad, but they are women . . .'[33]

Throughout the period during which the newly emerging Irish state was going through its difficult labour pains,

30 Paper given by Dr Margaret O'hÓgartaigh, *Sectarianism, Sexuality and Sterilisation at St Ultan's* at WERRC, University College Dublin, 8 April 2000.

31 Kathleen Lynn's Diaries, 1919–1955.

32 Various diary entries refer to Maud Gonne, Madeleine and later Charlotte Despard and their 'goat milk scheme for the babies', an attempt to provide the children with alternative healthy sustenance. Louie Bennett is noted as having fundraised for the hospital on her various trips to the United States, likewise Kathleen Clarke, who also sat on its Board. Andrée Sheehy Skeffington recounted a story of Hanna visiting the hospital and almost tripping over Constance, down on her knees scrubbing the floor. All of these individual women are mentioned in connection with St Ultan's over the course of Kathleen's diaries.

33 Alf McLochlinn and Andrée Sheehy Skeffington, *Writers, Raconteurs and Notable Feminists, Monographs* (Dublin, 1993) pp. 47–49.

Kathleen's diaries show how she spent her already overstretched time: promoting the political campaigns of the day and adding to the visibility and voice of Irishwomen. Yet alongside everything else, with Madeleine, Kathleen never ceased to meet the never-ending financial, emotional and clinical demands of the hospital and its vulnerable patients. As the years wore on and the promises embraced by the 1916 Proclamation were diluted and finally betrayed, her energies shifted and it was the latter commitment that prevailed over all else.

## Kathleen's Militant Republicanism

There is a particular perception of Kathleen as a woman whose profession alone was the cause of her presence within the arena of armed resistance. Diana Norman reflects this view when she describes Kathleen thus:

> Her name bobs up again and again like some merciful lifeboat, looking after jailed suffragettes, hunger-strikers, tending to the wounded and dying during the Easter Rising and, in 1919 founding St Ultan's Hospital . . .[34]

Andrée Sheehy Skeffington voices the more sentimental aspect of that perception in her reminiscences of Kathleen:

> . . . her medical bag was said to have contained a revolver (during Easter Week 1916), but one doubts that she would ever have used it. She was comforting a dying man on the roof of City Hall when the surrender came.[35]

Undoubtedly, her profession as a physician has given rise to assumptions about the extent of Kathleen's role in the military struggle for national liberation. It has been easier to accept Markievicz's military aggression as the actions of an aristocratic maverick or those of a singular individual than to consider that other women – women of education, breeding even – might harbour similar enthusiasms for combat. There is some truth to

34 Diana Norman, *Terrible Beauty*, p. 114.

35 McLochlinn and Sheehy Skeffington, *Monographs*.

Norman's description of Kathleen's constant duty of care to those she was close to and her political comrades in general. In the same way that Markievicz provided her particular skills of leadership and courage, Kathleen contributed her considerable talents as a physician. She was, however, an officer in a self-appointed 'standing' army, the Irish Citizen Army, and as such played her full part in military actions. Taillon recounts that in 1915, during preparations for the Rising, Kathleen used her car to transport arms (which were later discovered to be fakes) from a raid on the British Auxiliary Defence Force in Sutton.[36]

Her work as a doctor was equally as valuable as that of any fighting member of the ICA, but as an officer she also had a role as a military leader. This is most evident in Dublin Castle after the death of Sean Connolly. If Kathleen's role was only that of medical support, why then did she not urge surrender with his death? Instead, as the surviving next in command, she continued the attack against British Forces for some hours afterwards. The Sheehy Skeffington comment is inaccurate. Kathleen was not on the roof comforting a dying man – that incident had occurred hours before. Rather she was co-ordinating the attack when the sheer force of enemy numbers forced the unit to surrender. In addition, Sheehy Skeffington's doubts about Kathleen not being disposed towards using her revolver run counter to what would have been expected of her as an officer. Simply because there is no documented evidence to the contrary does not prove that Kathleen neither used her revolver nor was prepared to use it.

Kathleen can appear a mass of contradictions, but close attention to her diaries provides evidence of her consistency with regard to her commitment to armed struggle. Throughout the years of the War of Independence and the Civil War she 'keeps score' of victories won by Republicans against the British and the Pro-Treaty forces respectively.[37] In July and August of 1922 fierce fighting between Pro and Anti-Treatyists in Waterford resulted in a call for doctors to the area. Kathleen, in the midst of all her other commitments at St Ultan's, spent almost three

---

36 Taillon, *The Women of 1916*, p. 17.
37 Kathleen Lynn's Diaries, 1920–23.

weeks on the Anti-Treaty lines and the diary entries reflect the depth of her interest in military activity:

> Wed. a long day with little food and no rest last night or to-day. We beat off enemy 3 times, heavy fighting along 25 mile front, Slievenamon in it, our men in fine positions. They shelled us with trench mortars and all kinds of machine guns and we had one sl. [slightly] wounded in leg only. They lost many, killed and wounded and retreated at last.[38]

There is no doubt about Kathleen's compassion for the vulnerable in society and her fulfilment of her duty to care as a physician; but neither compassion nor caring obligations prevented her from actively supporting military action in support of a cause she believed in.

## Independence and Civil War 1920–1923

Whilst Republicanism was consolidating and reorganising under one banner, the Irish Women Worker's Union was re-establishing itself under a new general secretary, Louie Bennett.[39] Kathleen and her friends were engaged in prisoner support organisations, fund-raising and assisting in the work of developing St Ultan's, or active in Cumann na mBan, which had taken on a new lease of life under the presidency of Markievicz.[40] However, the fortunes of the Irish Citizen Army were not so productive. Splits within Liberty Hall, home of the radical labour movement and the Irish Transport and General Workers Union, combined with the loss of an irreplaceable leader, had taken their toll on the ICA's morale. By 1919, the ICA was riven with internal tensions, unsure of its role and without a political analysis.[41]

A reading of the only surviving minute book of the organisation reveals a group obsessed with the detail and rituals of

38 *Ibid.*, 2 May 1922.

39 Jones, *These Obstreperous Lassies.*

40 Ward, *Unmanageable Revolutionaries*, pp. 119–155.

41 Nevin, 'The Irish Citizen Army' in *James Larkin: Lion of the Fold.*

drilling, mobilising, mock manoeuvres, obtaining uniforms, band practices and holding endless court martials to hear charges and counter charges thrown at one another.[42] Kathleen's involvement had become peripheral and almost wholly related to innoculating ICA members and their families against influenza. At the organisation's AGM at the start of 1920, Kathleen and Madeleine were proposed in their absence for seats on the Army Council. The Secretary of the Council is dispatched to make the offer to them and the reply was minuted as: 'Sec. reported Miss ffrench-Mullen would act on new council if elected, Dr Lynn would not.'[43] Her decline of the offer to become an ICA council member may also have been influenced by the fact that earlier that year she had indeed joined the council, Dublin Corporation.

Local government elections in January 1920 swept a large number of Sinn Féin candidates into local councils, among them Kathleen for Rathmines and Madeleine for Harold's Cross.[44] On hearing the news of the successful election of both women, Tom Jacob, brother of Republican suffragist Rosamund Jacob, cheerfully commented, 'Rathmines won't know itself with Dr Lynn and Ms. ffrench-Mullen helping to rule its destinies.'[45] Kathleen lost no time in taking her place on the Public Health Committee, the Housing Committee and later the Milk Committee of the Council.

Yet all of these activities and her continuing Trojan work for St Ultan's occurred against a backdrop of unrelenting British coercion. Much of the country was under martial law, Sinn Féin and Cumann na mBan were proscribed organisations, and the vast majority of armed Republicans, now known as the Irish Republican Army, were on the run, jailed or in small guerrilla units attempting to engage the British military.[46] The treatment

---

42 Minute Book of the Council of the Irish Citizen Army, 1999–1920, Irish Labour History Museum.

43 *Ibid.*, 3 February 1920.

44 Kathleen Lynn's Diaries, January 1920.

45 Leah Levenson and Jerry Natterstad, *Hanna Sheehy Skeffington: Irish Feminist*, (Syracuse, 1987) p. 133.

46 Macardle, *The Irish Republic.*

of Irish prisoners and the devastation wrought by military raids, arrests, killings and destruction of property had attracted international attention and condemnation, in great part due to the lobbying and publicity done by Irish women activists.[47] The Irish White Cross, of which Kathleen was an active member, was all that stood between prisoners' families and destitution, that organisation having raised over £1.5 million between its formation at the end of 1920 and the summer of 1922.[48]

Kathleen's diaries for this period provide a detailed picture of mass round-ups, shootings, arrests of her women friends and raids on their homes. By Easter 1920 and the fourth anniversary of the Rising she comments, 'Couldn't do much for anniversary, we're so downtrodden now'.[49] Curfews in Dublin also seriously impeded Kathleen's work in the hospital and her ability to make rounds on her patients as a G.P. Her own home, where she also held her surgery,[50] was raided several times in 1920; but one of the most personally traumatic incidents was Madeleine's arrest by the notorious Black and Tans for 'spying'. The case against her was eventually dismissed, but the event had given Kathleen 'a fearful fright'.[51]

The introduction of the Better Government of Ireland Act by Lloyd George in May 1921 summoned into being two separate parliaments for the island, located in the six counties of the North and the 26 counties respectively. The Northern Parliament was entitled to send 13 representatives to Westminster and the 26 counties were entitled to 33 Westminster seats. Sinn Féin refused to recognise this partitionist solution or any attempt to continue under another guise with the implementation of Home Rule. Instead, it announced that the forthcoming elections decreed under the Act should be regarded as elections to the Second Dáil Éireann and an Anti-Partitionist plebiscite.

47 Ward, *Hannah Sheehy Skeffington.*

48 Ward, *Unmanageable Revolutionaries*, p. 148.

49 Kathleen Lynn's Diaries, 24 April 1920.

50 Ruane, *Ten Dublin Women*, p. 63 recounts how Kathleen would disguise herself as a well-dressed lady in a feather boa in order to do housecalls, thereby escaping detection by the security forces.

51 Kathleen Lynn's Diaries, 21–23 February 1920.

Sinn Féin won 124 seats out of a total of 128 in the Southern election and even in the North, where fierce violence from mobs of Orangemen and police towards Republican election organisers had dominated the campaigns, nationalists and Republicans won almost a quarter of the 52 seats.[52] Kathleen and Helena Molony had weathered the worst of northern Orangeism to work on the election campaign in Derry, which her diary described as an 'armed camp'.[53] The election in the South brought five new women deputies to join Constance Markievicz in the Dáil, all of them related to dead Republican leaders: Margaret Pearse, Ada English, Kathleen Clarke, Mary MacSwiney and Kate O'Callaghan.[54]

These results eventually forced Lloyd George into a Peace Conference with de Valera. Republicans rejoiced at this news, feeling that they were nearing victory and the closing of a deal that would lead to the establishment of the Irish Republic, and so a truce was declared. There is strong evidence of Kathleen's closeness to the Sinn Féin leadership at this time; shortly after the calling of the truce Kathleen's diary notes that she had 'tea with Dev and Griffith'.[55] Frustratingly, she makes no mention of what they discussed. The following months of the summer and autumn of that year saw a flurry of activity between Ireland and Britain, and the rejection of proposals offered by Britain. A protracted correspondence was conducted between de Valera and Lloyd George, including a series of secret meetings between representatives acting on their behalf. Finally, grounds were agreed on which to hold treaty negotiations. De Valera did not take part in these, sending instead Arthur Griffith and Michael Collins amongst others. The agreement that was eventually signed recognised the partition of Ireland and accepted an oath of allegiance to the Crown as entry for elected representatives to an Irish parliament. This Treaty became the basis for the terrible events of the Irish Civil War. Kathleen's reaction to the treaty is one of her most emotive diary entries:

52 Macardle, *The Irish Republic*, p. 417.

53 Kathleen Lynn's Diaries, 21–23 May 1921.

54 Ward, *Unmanageable Revolutionaries*, p. 153.

55 Kathleen Lynn's Diaries 8 July 1921.

Plate 8. Dáil Éireann Meeting, Mansion House, August 1921. *Courtesy of National Library of Ireland.*

> 'PEACE' terms but such a peace! Not what Connolly, Mallin and countless others died for. Please God the country won't agree to what Griffith, Barton, Gavan Duffy, Duggan and Mick Collins have put their names to, more shame them, better war than such a peace . . .[56]

Women's opposition to the Treaty was overwhelming nevertheless, the Republican movement was split along pro- and anti-Treaty lines.[57] The Dáil held several sessions with positions on each side becoming increasingly entrenched. By the end of that year, Kathleen's despondency is tangible, with even her infant patients in St Ultan's failing in health. Her final entry for 1921 reads, 'The year end is trying, uncertainty'.[58]

During the Civil War Kathleen's energies were severely tested. She was engaged in promoting the Republican cause, serving with the Republican forces in Waterford whilst her home and even the hospital was raided, and she arrested and pursued by her former comrades-in-arms.[59] 'Free Staters', as the pro-

56 *Ibid.*, 7 December 1921.

57 Ward, *In Their Own Voice*, pp. 111–118.

58 Kathleen Lynn's Diaries, 31 December 1921.

59 Kathleen's diaries over the Civil War period contain numerous references

Treatyists came to be known, embarked on a campaign of persecution against Republicans with executions, starvation of Republican prisoners, assaults on their families, and the introduction of legislation that conferred the 'death penalty for nearly everything'.[60] By May 1923, Republican resistance had been crushed, 'by means far more drastic than any which the British Government dared to impose during the worst period of the Rebellion.'[61] After heavy losses on both sides, including many of the leading figures, Republican forces declared a ceasefire. An election was called in August, for Treatyites were confident it would provide their mandate. Eighty-seven of the Republican candidates were in jail (de Valera was arrested whilst addressing an election meeting in Clare), or on the run. Nevertheless, Republicans won 44 seats, the Treaty side 63 and the remainder went to Labour and Independents.[62] Kathleen was returned for Dublin North, elected a member of an Irish Parliament in which she would never take her seat. She heard of her election success from the milkman.[63] Despite the fact that the war was over for Republicans, arrests continued and thousands of Republicans still remained imprisoned. A mass hunger strike ensued, lasting 41 days; but only after several deaths did the prisoners eventually gain their freedom, among them 51 women hunger-strikers.[64] Kathleen, who had made every effort to give them medical attention and to plead for their freedom, witnessed their eventual release, commenting that they were in 'bad condition, hardly able to stand'.[65] Sheila Humphries, a member of Cumann na mBan who had stayed 31 days on hunger strike, described the releases and the end of what was essentially the last concerted act of resistance by Republicans thus; 'We were flattened . . . The tinted trappings of our fight were hanging like rags about us.'[66]

---

to Collins and Richard Mulcahy and her personal sense of betrayal by them.

60 Kathleen Lynn's Diaries, 18 January 1923.

61 Macardle, *The Irish Republic*, p. 785.

62 *Ibid.*, pp. 788–789.

63 Diaries, 30 August 1923.

64 Ward, *Unmanageable Revolutionaries*, p. 148.

65 *Ibid.*, November-December 1923.

66 Cited in Ward, *Unmanageable Revolutionaries*, p. 148.

It was only a matter of time before de Valera found a formula that would allow him to enter into government in the new Free State.[67] In March 1926, he called a special Sinn Féin Ard Fheis. His motive was to put a proposal to the organisation to dedicate itself to campaigning to remove the oath of allegiance to Britain, a prerequisite to sitting in the new Dáil. Dev called for a new focus on constitutional means of dismantling the Treaty and away from Sinn Féin's abstentionist policy. He won by a narrow majority of five. Again the party was split, but there was no taste for acrimonious dispute left. Kathleen, Mary MacSwiney and Maíre Comerford of Cumann na mBan opposed the proposition; Constance, Hanna Sheehy Skeffington and Kathleen Clarke amongst others supported de Valera.[68] It was a case of agreeing to differ. De Valera took his remaining followers into a new party, Fianna Fáil, where the dilution of the 1916 vision continued unabated, with women paying the highest price of all. Sinn Féin staggered on and a further Ard Fheis was held in October of 1926 where, in a triumph of hope over reality, Kathleen and Madeleine put forward proposals on feeding schemes for children, house-building and education. These were agreed by an organisation without the political wherewithal to accomplish any plan of action.[69]

Kathleen's opposition to de Valera's 1926 proposal may not have been driven solely by her resistance to any compromise on the Treaty. Scattered throughout the Civil War years of the diaries are entries which betray a fluctuating belief in de Valera's leadership and politics. Feminists had concerns about de Valera's commitment to the principles contained in the Proclamation of Independence – in particular its assertion of equal opportunities for women and men – from at least 1916, when his was the only command during the Rising that refused the assistance of women. Hanna Sheehy Skeffington once wrote of

67 Kathleen Clarke, *Revolutionary Woman*, pp. 207–210. Clarke takes credit in her autobiography for initiating and 'persuading' de Valera into mounting a campaign to remove the oath of allegiance. Unsurprisingly, Macardle attributes it to de Valera's own ingenuity.

68 Ward, *Hanna Sheehy Skeffington*, p. 218.

69 Ward, *Unmanageable Revolutionaries*, pp. 203–204.

him that he showed 'mawkish distrust of women that has always coloured his outlook.'[70]

Immediately after the terms of the Treaty had become clear, Kathleen wrote to de Valera to remind him of his previous speech at the Sinn Féin Ard Fheis of 1921, where he had completely refuted the acceptance of allegiance to Britain as part of any agreement that might be negotiated between the two islands.[71] In doing so, Kathleen appeared to have had some doubt about de Valera's steadfastness on the issue. Perhaps, his failure to take part personally in the final negotiations with the British Government raised questions about his motivations. By letting Collins and the other delegates take responsibility for signing up to a deal that he knew to be inevitable, de Valera could remain untainted by the perceived betrayal of Republican principles involved. Those who did sign up to the agreement on behalf of the Republican movement were regarded as traitors, as Kathleen's entry on that subject shows. Dev's rejection of the Treaty a few days later succeeds in winning back Kathleen's loyalty: '. . . he is wonderful, very highly strung now, but strong and steadfast, how the man has come on, he is the Gideon I have been praying for since 1916.'[72] But her view of de Valera as a hero of biblical proportions has sufficiently eroded by 1923 when she comments, 'Dev is very mad at me because I criticised him'.[73] She does not elucidate as to why this might be but about this period, Dev had been attempting to find endorsement from Republicans for an unconditional surrender. Such a move would have been unthinkable to Kathleen, as it was to many others, and she might well have told him so. If she was uncertain about his political commitment to core Republican beliefs, then perhaps his 1926 proposal did not come as such a shock to her. Having survived the human tragedy of civil war, she felt no bitterness towards those of her friends and comrades who were willing to support de Valera's proposition. Certainly, her friendship and support to those women who disagreed with her and

70 Quoted from *In Their Own Voice*, p. 165.
71 Kathleen Lynn's Diaries, 8 December 1921.
72 *Ibid.*, 13 December 1921.
73 *Ibid.*, 21 February 1923.

left Sinn Féin at that time remained steadfast. Her relationship with de Valera, however, continued to disintegrate, and by the time of the 1937 Constitution she had nothing but contempt for him and his party.[74] Kathleen actively campaigned with other women activists against the Constitution, commenting in her diary, 'Mrs Kettle[75] says she works day & night with protest against new Constitution's rule for women, of course they are reactionary.'[76] Typically, on the day of the vote, she and Madeleine 'Voted early. We put No for Constitution & Restore the Republic on voting paper.'[77]

From 1926 onwards, in the context of what Kathleen perceived as de Valera's betrayal of Republican ideals, her involvement with politics is one of an informed enthusiast otherwise engaged. Building St Ultan's into a respected medical institution and pioneering radical approaches to children's healthcare became her consuming preoccupation. She did, however, as one would expect given her previous track record within nationalist politics, take a stand with those remaining feminists who fought de Valera's 1937 Constitution.[78] The 'revolver' that symbolised her past life was put away and she spent the rest of her life championing the rights of her young patients against a complacent Catholic medical system.[79] In her pursuit of justice, Dr Kathleen Lynn never 'disarmed'.

---

74 *Ibid.*, 10 May 1937.

75 Mary Kettle, a sister of Hanna Sheehy Skeffington, was the widow of an Irish Party MP and, although a feminist, had supported the Irish Party rather than Sinn Féin in the 1918 election.

76 *Ibid.*, 13 May 1937.

77 *Ibid.*, 1 July 1937.

78 Women's resistance to the 1937 Constitution is covered in a number of texts. See works already cited by Ward, Clarke and Jones. Also, for details of the social, political and economic impact of the Free State on women from 1922–1937 see Mary E. Daly, 'Women in the Irish Free State, 1922–1939: The Interaction between Economics and Ideology' and Maryann Valiulis, 'Power, Gender and Identity in the Irish Free State', both in Joan Hoff and Maureen Coulter (eds), *Irish Women's Voices, Past and Present, Journal Of Women's History*, Vol. 6 No. 4/Vol. 7 No. 1 (Indiana, 1995) pp. 99–136.

79 O'hÓgartaigh, *Sex, Sectarianism, Sexuality and Sterilisation at St Ultan's.*

# Chapter 5

## CONCLUSION

It has been the aim of this book to explore some of the private and very human relationships that shaped Kathleen's life as a means to better understand the political choices and decisions she made. This approach to the history of Kathleen Lynn has been influenced by the writings of Gerda Lerner and her belief that:

> Being human means thinking and feeling; it means reflecting on the past and visioning into the future. We experience; we give voice to that experience; others reflect on it and give it new form. That new form, in its turn, influences and shapes the way next generations experience their lives. That is why history matters.[1]

Kathleen Lynn never wrote a polemic when a few brisk sentences would do. She does not appear to have been an orator or a woman of letters; rather, she is a woman for whom actions spoke louder than words. In this latter respect, she was not unlike her friend Constance Markievicz. Like Constance she also made alliances across many different organisations, amongst them the IWSLGA, Inghinidhe na hÉireann, the IWFL, the ICA, the IWWU, Cumann na mBan, Cumann na dTeachtaire and Sinn Féin. Some of her alliances were based on expediency and a need to take quick action in redressing the causes of social injustice. Other longer-term involvements were the practical articulation of deeply held beliefs in women's equality and Republicanism. My growing awareness and knowledge of these

1 Gerda Lerner, *Why History Matters, Life and Thought* (Oxford and New York, 1997) p. 211.

aspects of Kathleen has strengthened my perception of her as a rebel in the most enduring sense.

The usage of the term 'rebel' is one most often associated with an Irish nationalist fervour that is consistently masculine. Carol Coulter argues that the conception of freedom and independence held by the majority of Irish nationalist male leaders never challenged the economic and social fundamentals of the patriarchal British state they sought to overthrow, and instead 'posited independence in terms of replacing that state with an Irish replica of it . . . Many were more interested in the outward signs of independence.'[2] Kathleen's actions and involvements were consistent with a 'rebel' outlook that went beyond the narrow agenda of her male comrades. The establishment of rights for women, children and the poor was the motivation for her involvement in Republicanism and remained her central objective, always dictating the course of action she took. Kathleen, and the other women of 1916, to a greater extent than any of their male compatriots manifested a 'rebel' nature that went to the heart of what Irish freedom required. Hence, their opposition to a treaty that provided only for an exchange of power without challenging existing relations of power within Ireland.

Towards the end of the political period under scrutiny, I believe that Kathleen had begun to consciously reshape her immediate environment and to shift her energies without compromising her strong Republican beliefs. Republicanism had reorganised, split, gone to war with itself, and re-emerged with its original ideological focus overwhelmed. Kathleen, on the other hand, refused to lose sight of the core values that drove her and embarked on a course of action that allowed her to be true to those values in a more directly fulfilling way. It took her away from the centre of political activity where she had operated for almost two decades, but not from those individuals whom she most trusted. Her love for them and their support for her continued throughout the long project that was St Ultan's Hospital.

---

2 Carol Coulter, *The Hidden Tradition, Feminism, Women and Nationalism* (Cork, 1993) p. 22.

Kathleen Lynn had none of the credentials that were usually attached to the few women whose names are recollected in connection with early twentieth-century Republicanism. She was not a patriot's widow or other female relative. She did not come from a nationalist dynasty. Her Republican politics were not posited in relation to any man, but were the independent choice of an autonomous woman. It has become almost a credo of historical faith to discount the presence of women within Republican ranks as women in thrall to their menfolk. Constance Markievicz is often regarded as an eccentric exception to that rule, but she was not alone. Kathleen and many of her women friends adhered to a Republicanism that embraced their belief in women's equality, justice and freedom. The failure to make manifest those aspirations lies with the narrowness of men's political vision and their resistance to sharing power with women. The opportunity to harness the abilities and talents of women like Kathleen Lynn in the creation of the Irish Republic was squandered, and our legacy as a state is diminished as a result.

# Bibliography


Alberti, Johanna, *Beyond Suffrage: Feminists in War and Peace, 1914–1928* (Macmillan, Basingstoke, 1998)

Alpern, Sara; Antler, Joyce; Perry, Elisabeth; and Scobie, Ingrid, *The Challenge of Feminist Biography* (University of Illinois Press, Chicago, 1992)

Beddoe, Deirdre, *Discovering Women's History, A Practical Guide to Researching the Lives of Women Since 1800* (Longman, London, New York, 1998)

Clancy, Mary, 'Aspects of Women's Contribution to the Oireachtas Debates in the Irish Free State, 1922–37' in Maria Luddy and Cliona Murphy (eds), *Women Surviving, Studies in Irish Women's History in the 19th and 20th Centuries* (Poolbeg Press, Dublin, 1990)

Clarke, Kathleen, *My Fight for Ireland's Freedom* (The O'Brien Press Ltd, Dublin, 1991)

Connolly, Nora, *The Irish Rebellion of 1916 or The Unbroken Tradition* (Boni and Liveright, New York, 1919)

Coulter, Carol, *The Hidden Tradition: Feminism, Women and Nationalism in Ireland* (Cork University Press, Cork, 1993)

Cullen, Mary (ed.), *Irish Women in Education in the 19th and 20th Centuries* (Argus Press, Dublin,1987)

Cullen, Mary, and Luddy, Maria (eds), *Female Activists: Irish Women and Change 1900–1960* (The Woodfield Press, Dublin, 2001)

Cullen Owens, Rosemary, *Smashing Times, A History of the Irish Women's Suffrage Movement 1889–1922* (Attic Press, Dublin, 1984)

Donoghue, Emma, *Passions Between Women, British Lesbian Culture 1668–1801* (Scarlet Press, London, 1993)

Duberman, Martin Bauml; Vicinus, Martha; and Chauncey, George (eds), *Hidden from History: Reclaiming Gay and Lesbian Past* (Penguin Books, London, 1989)

Faderman, Lilian, *Surpassing the Love of Men* (The Women's Press, London, 1985)

Fox, R. M., *The Green Banners: The Story of the Irish Struggle* (Secker and Warburg, London, 1938)

Gray, Breda, and Ryan, Louise, '(Dis)Locating "Woman" and Women in Representations of Irish Nationality' in Byrne, Anne, and Leonard, Madeleine (eds), *Women and Irish Society, A Sociological Reader* (Beyond The Pale Publications, Belfast, 1997)

Gifford, Sydney, *The Years Flew By* (Gifford and Craven, Dublin, 1974)

Griffith, Kenneth, and O'Grady, Timothy, *Ireland's Unfinished Revolution: An Oral History* (Robert Rinehart Publishers, Niwot, 1998)

Hamer, Emily, *Britannia's Glory: A History of Twentieth-Century Lesbians* (Cassell, London, 1996)

Hart, Ellen Louise, and Smith, Martha Nell (eds), Open Me Carefully: Emily Dickinson's Intimate Letters to Susan Huntington Dickinson (Paris Press, Ashfield, MA, 1998)

Hoff, Joan, and Coulter, Moureen (eds), 'Irish Women's Voices: Past and Present' *Journal of Women's History*, Vol 6, No 4 / Vol 7, No 1, Winter/Spring 1995

Jones, Mary, *These Obstreperous Lassies: A History of the Irish Women Workers Union, 1889–1922* (Gill and Macmillan, Dublin, 1984)

Kostick, Conor, and Collins, Lorcan, *The Easter Rising: A Guide to Dublin in 1916* (O'Brien Press, Dublin, 2000)

Lerner, Gerda, *Why History Matters* (Oxford University Press, New York and Oxford, 1997)

Lesbian History Group, *Not a Passing Phase: Reclaiming Lesbians in History, 1840–1985* (The Women's Press, London, 1989)

Levenson, Leah, and Natterstad, Jerry H., *Hanna Sheehy Skeffington* (Syracuse University Press, Syracuse, 1986)

Lewis, Gifford, *Eva Gore-Booth and Esther Roper – A Biography* (Pandora, London, 1988)

Lyons, J.B., *Brief Lives of Irish Doctors* (Blackwater, Dublin, 1978)

Macardle, Dorothy, *The Irish Republic* (Corgi, London, 1968)

McCoole, Sinéad, *Guns and Chiffon, Women Revolutionaries and Kilmainham Gaol* (Stationery Office, Dublin, 1997)

McLochlinn, Alf, and Sheehy Skeffington, Andrée, *Writers, Raconteurs and Notable Feminists, Monographs* (National Library of Ireland, Dublin, 1993)

Meaney, Geraldine, 'Sex and Nation: Women in Irish Culture and Politics' in *A Dozen Lips* (Attic Press, Dublin, 1994)

Mulvihill, Margaret, *Charlotte Despard: A Biography* (Pandora, London, 1989)

Murphy, Clíona, 'The Tune of the Stars and Stripes: The American Influence on the Irish Suffrage Movement' in Maria Luddy and Clíona Murphy (eds), *Women Surviving, Studies in Irish Women's History in the 19th and 20th Centuries* (Poolbeg Press, Dublin, 1990)

Murphy, Clíona, *The Women's Suffrage Movement and Irish Society in the Twentieth Century* (Harvester/Wheatsheaf, London, 1989)

Nevin, Donal, 'The Irish Citizen Army, 1913–1916' in Nevin, Donal, *James Larkin: Lion of the Fold* (Gill and Macmillan in association with RTÉ and SIPTU, Dublin, 1998)

Norman, Diana, *Terrible Beauty. A Life of Constance Markievicz* (Poolbeg Press, Dublin, 1987)

O'Connor, Anne V., and Parkes, Susan M., *Gladly Learn and Gladly Teach: A History of Alexandra College and School, Dublin 1866–1966* (Blackwater Press, Dublin, 1984)

Rowbotham, Sheila, *A Century of Women* (Viking, London and New York, 1997)

Rowbotham, Sheila, *A New World of Women: Stella Browne – Socialist Feminist* (Pluto Press, London, 1977)

Ruane, Medb, *Ten Dublin Women* (Women's Commemoration and Celebration Committee, Dublin, 1991)

Ryan, Louise, *Irish Feminism and The Vote, An Anthology of the Irish Citizen Newspaper 1912–1920* (Folens, Dublin, 1996)

Ryan, W.P., *The Irish Labour Movement* (Talbot Press, Dublin, 1919)

Smyth, Hazel P., 'Kathleen Lynn, M.D. FRCSI' in *Dublin Historical Record*, 30, (Dublin, 1997)

Taillon, Ruth, *When History Was Made, The Women of 1916* (Beyond the Pale Publications, Belfast, 1996)

Valiulis, Maryann Gialanella, 'Power, Gender and Identity in the Irish Free State' in Joan Hoff and Moureen Coulter (eds), *Irish Women's Voices Past and Present, Journal of Women's History* Vol. 6 No. 4 / Vol. 7 No. 1 Winter/Spring 1995 (Indiana University Press, Indiana, 1995)

Vicinus, Martha, ' "They Wonder to Which Sex I Belong". The Historical Routes of Modern Lesbian Identity' in Altman, Denis, *Which Homosexuality?* (Gay Men's Press, London, 1989)

Ward, Margaret, *Hannah Sheehy Skeffington, A Life* (Attic Press, Dublin, 1997)

Ward, Margaret, *In Their Own Voice, Women and Irish Nationalism* (Attic Press, Dublin, 1995)

Ward, Margaret, 'The League of Women Delegates and Sinn Féin 1917' in *History Ireland*, Vol. 4, No. 3, Autumn 1996

Ward, Margaret, 'The Missing Sex: Putting Women into Irish History' in *A Dozen Lips* (Attic Press, Dublin, 1994)

Ward, Margaret, *Unmanageable Revolutionaries* (Pluto Press, London, 1983)

# INDEX

Index

## Index